D1093390

45,12

OPEN YOUR OWN SALON...
THE RIGHT WAY!

The complete step by step guide to planning, launching and managing your own salon business!

EGO IWEGBU-DALEY

Published by Agushka Publishing, London

Agushka Publishing

+44 (0) 845 643 1619

First Edition 2008

© Copyright 2008 Ego Iwegbu-Daley

THOMAS DANBY
COLLEGE
LEARNING CENTRE - LIBRARY

CLASS NO	646.7206 IWE
ACC. NO.	022782

All rights reserved. No part of this publication may be reproduced, stored in or introduced into a retrieval system, or transmitted, in any form, or by any means (electronic, mechanical, photocopying, recording or otherwise) without the prior written permission of the publisher.

This book is sold subject to the condition that it shall not, by way of trade or otherwise, be lent, resold, hired out, or otherwise circulated without the publishers prior consent in any form of binding or cover other than that in which it is published and without a similar condition including this condition being imposed on the subsequent purchaser.

The Open Your Own Salon... The Right Way! handbook is meant for general information purposes only. Following it does not guarantee success in your business venture. Agushka Publishing, Miss Salon™ and Ego Iwegbu-Daley will accept no responsibility for any outcome or liabilities which may arise in relation to any use of or reliance on the information provided.

ISBN
978-0-9560351-2-7
Open Your Own Salon...The Right Way!(Paperback)

Content

Introduction

Hi and congratulations on choosing to buy this handbook and save yourself a lot of time, money and chaos that can happen at the start of any business due purely to lack of experience. Even if you already own a salon, you will find this handbook very useful as it is full of tips on improving your income, staff management and raising finance for expansion or new equipment.

Why Use This Book?

If you are new to business it can be easy to make many unnecessary and often costly mistakes. This Open Your Own Salon... The Right Way! handbook will attempt to guide you through the entire planning and implementation stages of launching your own salon business and beyond; highlighting many crucial areas that may not be so obvious when you start out but become problems down the line.

This book is a guide; full of do's and don'ts, examples, useful tips and where to go for more relevant information. It also takes you through how to prepare and present the dreaded business plan, step by step!

It starts with an 20-Step Action Plan, guiding you on what to do and when, and ends with a Check List, ensuring that all the important stuff has been completed before you open the doors to your wonderful new business! You will know upfront what is required of you, be shown tried and tested techniques and feel confident that you won't be faced with nasty surprises that could have easily been avoided.

It is mostly targeted to a UK audience but still very useful to anyone around the world.

About Ego Iwegbu-Daley

Ego opened her first salon in 1999. It was an open-plan nail bar in Topshop Oxford Circus, London; the first of its kind. Over the next 5 years, she went on to open a further 4 nail bars in Selfridges&Co London, Trafford, Manchester and Birmingham; a stand-alone salon in Fulham and countless beauty counters at various national shows for companies like Superdrug, Crabtree & Evelyn, Dorothy Perkins and more. Ego has a degree in Mathematics from Kings College London, has been a judge for the Professional Beauty awards, has a regular column in an industry magazine and has successfully completed a number of other business ventures.

Personal experience has driven her to write this handbook.

❝ So many people start businesses and fail at the first hurdle due to lack of knowledge and guidance. I wish I had a business mentor when I first started out; especially one who was experienced in my specific business. In writing this book I am hoping to be your virtual mentor. The no nonsense, straight to the point, detailed approach I have taken should help you get your salon up and running with the least errors.

There are many very talented nail technicians, beauty therapists and hairdressers that have great organisational and people skills but don't go for their dream of being their own boss because they can't write a business plan or they worry about money, rules, regulations, and other obstacles that all seem insurmountable.

Starting a business, any business, is far from easy, but if you are focused, determined and have faith in your abilities, you too can overcome the hurdles and show your enterprising side.

I now run Miss Salon™, a Nail Bar and Salon Business Consultancy. We focus on helping aspiring salon owners make the right choices and cover all bases; turning their dream into reality!

I hope that when you finish reading this handbook, you will feel confident and motivated to go for it and open your own salon!

Acknowledgements and Thank You's

I would like to thank all the salon owners that took the time out of their busy days to speak with me and share their business experiences. Their stories allowed me to write not just from my own experiences and perspective, but also from theirs.

I would also like to thank all the wonderful people who have contacted Miss Salon with their enquiries, feedback and business dreams; you continue to inspire me and provide me with insights into the issues facing aspiring salon owners, helping me stay focused on what is important to you in this book.

Thank you also to my family for their never ending support and encouragement.

How To Use This Book

Throughout this handbook, as described below, I will use symbols to help highlight certain information...

Chapter Reference

The info symbol will point you to the right chapter

Action

Get it done when you see the target!

Example

See the square symbol when I'm giving an example

Ideas

Put your thinking cap on when you see the the light bulb!

Motivator

When stuff looks hard, I hope Smiley will keep you going!!

There is a 20-Step Action Plan, which is an overview of what you will need to do to go from idea to salon! This is followed by writing the Business Plan, which contains all the headings your plan will need, in the correct order, guidelines as to what to write under each heading, some examples and chapter references for more information.

The rest of the handbook goes into more detail on each aspect of setting up, launching and managing your business.

Keeping an eye on the Action Plan and Check List, start with the business plan on chapter 3 and, as instructed, use the chapter references to help you complete it.

For clarity, please read the handbook once from start to finish before you attempt the business plan.

Once your salon is open, refer back to your business plan to help you keep on the right track and make the most of your wonderful new business!

Get In Touch!

We would love to hear from you! Tell us about your business venture; how is it going for you, what have been your successes, what have been your nightmares!? We would also love to hear any feedback or comments you have about this handbook and any of our other business tools.

Please email misssalon@misssalon.com

GOOD LUCK!

Miss Salon™ Business Shop - www.**misssalonbusiness**.com

There are a number of salon-specific business tools available to purchase from Miss Salon™. See the list below and visit www.missssalon.com for more information.

A Completed Sample Business Plan £40.00* PDF
This is an actual business plan for a chain of nail bars that successfully raised £250k in loans and investment.

Sample Staff Handbook and Contract of Employment £9.99* PDF
Save yourself the time and effort of figuring out what to include and how to include it in your own staff handbook (employment manual); just tailor this sample to suit your salon!

Treatment and Product Pricing Calculator £24.99*
Microsoft Excel
This is an amazing Microsoft Excel spreadsheet; just input your salons direct and indirect costs and the calculator will work out what you need to charge for your services!

Profit & Loss Template £15.99* Microsoft Excel
Load your estimated or actual incomes and expenses into this template and it will create your P&L!

Cash Flow Template £15.99* Microsoft Excel
Just input what you spend, when you spend it and this dynamic template will keep you up-to-date on your cash situation. Also forecast your cash flow needs by including possible future spending.

Direct Costs Estimator Template £15.99* Microsoft Excel
Workout your businesses direct costs with this easy to use excel spreadsheet.

Health & Safety Policy Template £19.99* Microsoft Word
This is a H&S Policy used in a salon; just insert your business name and details into this template. Every salon must have a H&S Policy.

Health & Safety Procedure Manual Template £24.99*
Microsoft Word
This H&S Procedure Manual, specifically designed for a salon, will save you the time and stress of producing your own from scratch. It contains all the required headings and sample content which you can easily replace with relevant statements about your salon.

Sample Health & Safety Induction £9.99* PDF
This Health & Safety Induction agenda is an excellent example of how a salons induction training session should be conducted.

Staff Performance Review Questionnaire £3.99* Microsoft Word
A complete performance review document created to assist you in conducting, the all important, formal staff assessments.

Sample Recruitment Interview Questions £3.99* Microsoft Word
A list of questions to definitely ask during an interview

Salon Inspection Sheet £3.99* Microsoft Word
A full salon inspection sheet with 10 questions that cover everything from appearance, to organisation, to staff participation

To purchase these products please visit www.misssalonbusiness. com or telephone our order and advice line on +44 (0)845 643 1619. They are available either on a CD or via email.

*Prices may vary from those printed
All of the products are © Copyright 2008 Ego Iwegbu-Daley

Dedicated to my amazing son Boris and beautiful sleeping daughter Annabelle

Also, dedicated to all the people out there who just want to make it in business...

Don't give up; just keep on reaching!

Chapter 1
YOU, THE SALON OWNER

Being an Entrepreneur!

Creating something from nothing...

Starting your own business is like creating something from nothing... An idea comes to mind and starts to grow bigger and bigger in your thoughts. If you are passionate about it, it starts to take over your entire existence; you just can't stop thinking about it! Then with a huge amount of energy and commitment these thoughts turn into tangible assets - chairs, tables, a shop front, a reception desk, phone lines and hopefully customers! It really is creating something from nothing more than your energy and drive.

Make no mistake, starting and running your own business is tough, very tough. You will experience emotional extremes; super highs and frustrating lows! You will have to deal with rejection, stress, exhaustion and many moments of just wanting to give up, but if you are brave and determined nothing will stand in the way of you starting your own business! ☺ Not money (or the lack of), not self-doubt and not even negative people around you will stop you from getting there. And when you do, the personal and financial rewards make it all worth it!

Skills You Should Acquire To Get You Through...

So it is clear that the first set of characteristics required of an entrepreneur are drive, determination, resilience and courage. With these characteristics you will be able to acquire the other skills and abilities you will need to make a success of your business, these are:-

* Being a **good planner** and able to see the whole picture. Owning a salon business has many aspects to it; you will need to be able to establish all of these aspects and continuously view your business in its entirety, from staffing to marketing, from finance

---

i See chapter... ◎ Get it done ⚲ Thinking time ■ Example ☺ You can do it!

to maintaining hygiene. Prepare a business plan and make being a good planner easy.

- Being an **opportunist** and seizing the moment! The term opportunist generally comes across negatively but here I mean it in the best possible sense. There are times in business when rare and fantastic opportunities to progress or grab a good deal present themselves; you need to be able to recognise these moments and make the most of them! They could be the big break you've been waiting for.

- Being a **quick thinker and a fast learner**; you will constantly be bombarded with new information, whether it's a new treatment or a crisis in the salon; your ability to make good decisions, fast, will go a long way.

- Being a **hard worker**! I think it is quite important to point out at this stage the level of work required to get your business off the ground - A Lot! I can only relate it to the amount of work and change to your life that happens when you have a baby! Be prepared; eat well, stay hydrated and pop a few Vitamin C's when you remember!

- Being well **organised**; keep good records, create clearly labelled folders, always have a daily to-do list, calendar, diary and an up-to-date address book.

- Being able to **keep your eye on the prize**; Profit! You are in business to make money, hence your plans, operations and decisions should always be focused on the ultimate goal of sustained financial stability and growth. Make this easy by creating and maintaining cash-flow and profit & loss forecasts.

- Being a hands-on **good leader**; leading by example. Good leadership is a hugely important skill; harping out instructions at your team from a distance rarely ever gets good results. So, at least initially, you must be there, you must be present, you must be a patient guide and lead by example. Good leadership also includes planning well, thus insuring that overall the business keeps moving in the right direction.

- Able to **work really well under pressure** and when totally stressed out! This includes not panicking, losing your rag and having a calm exterior when required.

- Being a **great communicator**; you need to be able to instil enthusiasm in your listeners (investors, staff, suppliers and customers), motivate your team when times are hard, sell and generate revenue and more! If you think that your communication skills could do with a polishing then start by practising on your friends and family. Ask them to take on the role of an investor or a client and see if you can get them to buy into your idea or product... just keep practising!

- Being a **problem solver**; seeing problems as opportunities and never tire of looking for another way out.

- Able to take criticism and **continuously seek ways to improve** on your leadership techniques.

 ☺Don't be put off by this list... remember that even the most successful business people, including Richard Branson, Anita Roddick, Martha Stewart, Alan Sugar and James Dyson made mistakes!

Read this handbook, continue to seek advice and inspiration and think of the sense of achievement, pride and satisfaction you will gain from running your own business and being your own boss!

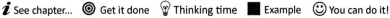

Chapter 2
THE 20-STEP ACTION PLAN

What's my next move?

The work begins...

Now as an aspiring entrepreneur, you need to develop your unique idea, construct a market analysis, assess the competition, create a sales and marketing plan, determine risks and rewards and then execute your plan! Please note that I said execute your plan; not idea or dream or thought; you must have a *well thought-out and thoroughly researched* **plan**.

So What's The Plan Then?

Use the below action plan to give you direction and help you stay on track of all your tasks. ☺ **Try to not overwhelm yourself by thinking of all the jobs at once!**

Step	◎ Action	Chapters
1	Do a Market Analysis (research). *Answer this:-* *Is there a market for your type of salon? What size is it; will there be enough business? How can you tailor your idea to better suit the clientele in the area?*	13
2	Start writing a business plan and using your research from step 1. Include financial projections and a sales and marketing plan. *Answer this: - Is the idea viable; can it make money?*	2, 5, 13
3	Find out what laws and other regulations will affect your business. In most places, salon and individual licenses are required to trade.	15

i See chapter...　◎ Get it done　💡 Thinking time　■ Example　☺ You can do it!

Step	◎ Action	Chapters
4	Confirm how much money/capital you will need. Start to seek financing if necessary.	14
5	Find an accountant, solicitor and graphics / web designer. *Keep updating your business plan.*	16
6	Register your company or if sole-trader or partnership, register for tax. Understand what all your tax obligations will be.	4, 14
7	Open a business bank account.	14
8	Complete on raising all the required funding	14
9	Seek and secure premises, design layout and hire shop-fitters. Look into furniture requirements. *Advertise salon in shop window!*	6
10	Staff; conclude on the number of staff you will need, their job roles and salaries. Plan the recruitment process including creating the employment and training manuals. Start advertising for staff.	7
11	Apply for salon license and get insurance.	15

Step	◎ Action	Chapters
12	Have a clear plan for how your business will operate and be managed, including payroll management, cleaning, rotas and more.	7-12
13	Interview, screen and hire staff.	7
14	Write a Health & Safety procedures manual including inductions and risk assessments.	15
15	Carefully create a treatment & product list.	5
16	Print price-lists and any other promotional material. *Keep updating your marketing plan.*	5, 13, 16
17	Keeping to budget, prepare your first stock list. Purchase stock. Purchase and fit all equipment.	8
18	Clean and merchandise shop and salon.	9, 10, 13
19	Welcome and train staff on-site.	7
20	Have an opening day and launch your wonderful salon!!!!!!	17

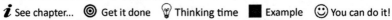

Chapter 3
THE BUSINESS PLAN

If you fail to plan, you plan to fail!

The dreaded business plan!

Well it's not *that* bad - just think of it as a way of telling the story of your business in writing. You don't need to have any special skills or years of experience to put together a good business plan; just the desire to be thorough and start your business the right way.

Whether you are seeking to raise money for your venture or are lucky enough to already have all the capital you need **writing a business plan is essential**; without it you'll be heading into a complex venture with no clear goals, no plan of action and no strategy for success. Once complete, your business and marketing plan will guide you through all the various aspects of setting-up and running your salon; giving you all the tools you need to target your market, control your finances, know your financial goals and how to achieve them.

At first writing the plan can seem like a chore but once you get into it, you'll be excited about all the great aspects of your business it highlights. It will also help you think through all the aspects that are not so clear. If you put your mind to it, you can write your plan quite quickly; especially if you follow my headings and guides below.

Plan now and save yourself running around like a headless chicken later, wasting time and money, wishing you had thought of this, remembered that and so on!

Always remember...

A successful business owner is a planner and a doer! Don't hide behind the business plan; I expect you to be out there, researching your idea, meeting suppliers, estate agents, bank managers and so on.

---

i See chapter... ◎ Get it done ♀ Thinking time ■ Example ☺ You can do it!

PRESENTING YOUR BUSINESS PLAN

Apart from using the business plan for your own direction and clarity, you may also want to use your plan to raise finance. Later, in chapter 14, Finance and Accounting, I discuss who to approach for financing; for now I want to focus on how to create and present the full business plan.

A full business plan can be lengthy and detailed and as such it is always a good idea to create an Executive Summary. This is a summary of key information lifted from the full business plan that allows potential investors to decide, at a glance, whether or not your business is one that may be of interest to them. Most experienced investors and lenders have certain criteria when deciding on a venture, for example, some don't invest in start-up businesses (new businesses) and only choose those that are already established, but require funding for expansion; others invest in start-ups, but only those that expect a certain turnover or require a certain level of funding. Some investors don't invest in the beauty or retail industry at all; others do. The list goes on but the point is that an executive summary can save everyone time and most experienced investors will ask to see one before the full business plan.

Business plans come in different shapes, sizes and formats depending on the industry and audience, but ultimately they all still have the same sort of information. The business plan format in this guide is one that I successfully used to raise £750K for my businesses. This format is made up of the following 6 sections:-

1. The executive summary (often sent separately from the rest)
2. The business; description and analysis
3. The marketing plan
4. Description of finances
5. Analysis of finance, financial statements and projections
6. Operations and processes

A detailed look at sections 2 to 6 will follow, but first let us look at what a typical executive summary should contain.

Remember that an executive summary is a summary of the key points in your full business plan and therefore is created AFTER the full plan has been written.

Section 1 - The Executive Summary

An executive summary for a one salon business should really be able to fit onto one or two pages and should contain at least the following information:-

Heading	Content
Title	Executive Summary for *[enter the name of the business]*.
Business Description	Enter summary of what the business intends to do.
Proposed Location	Enter where the salon/shop will be.
Projected Revenue	Enter the total yearly income, profit and profit margin estimates for the next 3/5 years.
Capital Expenditure	Enter amount needed to start the business.
Funds Requested	Enter the amount of money you are requesting from that particular investor or lender; is it a loan or investment, the rate of return and for what stake in the business.
Future Plans	Enter any exciting plans that you may have for the business.

i See chapter... ◎ Get it done ⑨ Thinking time ■ Example ☺ You can do it!

Heading	Content
Competitors	List who your competitors are and a little info about them.
Keys to Success	Enter the most important factors to ensuring the long-term success of the business, e.g. an excellent and experienced salon manager is vital to the success of the salon; a solid marketing plan could be a key factor; enthusiastic, experienced and qualified staff may also be key to the business. Think about and add what's vital for your business.
Contact Details	Enter details of who to contact for questions and more information.

Don't worry if you don't understand some of the information required at this stage; go on to produce the full business plan and once completed return to the executive summary, most things should be clear by then. Please note:- don't present the executive summary in a table format as above; rather use the headings as titles and enter the content underneath each title.

Chin up...

Not everyone is going to like you, your idea or your plan; be brave, be strong, stay focused and keep on improving and developing your idea until you get what you want!!!

THE FULL BUSINESS PLAN

Below are the headings for each section of the full business plan; we will look at each one in detail...

Section 2 – The Business

- Business name and logo
- Contact Details
- Business Structure
- Business Description
- Business History
- Revenue
- Services and Products
- The Management
- Staff Requirements
- Salon Premises
- The Shop-fit, Furniture and Decoration
- Suppliers
- Opening Hours
- Government Regulations
- SWOT Analysis

Section 3 – Marketing

- The Marketing Plan (summary)
- The Brand
- Uniqueness
- Customer Loyalty
- Competitor Analysis
- The Marketing Budget and Targets
- Schedule of Planned Promotional and Advertising Activities
- The Future

 *i* See chapter... Get it done Thinking time ■ Example ☺ You can do it!

Section 4 – Description of Finances

- Proposed Financing – How much money do you need?
- Ownership and Return-On-Investment (ROI)
- Use of Proceeds
- Reporting
- Investor Involvement
- Fees Paid

Section 5 - Analysis of Finance, Financial Statements and Projections

- Cash flow
- Profit and Loss
- Assumption and Other Calculations

Section 6 – Operations and Processes

- Recruitment Process
- Training Programme
- Stock Orders
- Quality Control
- Customer Complaints
- Salon Law and Order

Summary

- Business Plan Summary

So here we go...
Remember to follow the Action symbol ◎ and just
start writing... it's easy!

Section 2 - The Business

Business Name & Logo

What are you going to call your business? I think the best names are the ones that don't keep punters guessing as to what you do, however, this is up to you and there are arguments for and against this thinking. For example, Bliss, Cowshed, Sharps and Scarlet are all names of salons of one type or another; they are not descriptive but are great for standing-out of the crowd. Whilst Jessica's Beauty Salon is straight-to-the-point but maybe a little uninspiring! It all boils down to appealing to your target market - so knowing your intended target market will help you choose an appropriate name.

i **Read**
Chapter 13, Marketing

◎ **Action**
Decide on a name and write it at the start of your business plan, include your logo if you have one.

Contact Details

Let investors know how to get in touch with you and any other important people in your team.

i **Read**
Chapter 16, Professional Services

◎ **Action**
Write the following in your plan:-

- Your name.
- Registered office, shop address or another address where you can be reached.

- Telephone numbers and an email address.
- If known, include the names and contacts of your professional service providers - Accountant, Solicitor, Business bank account.

Business Structure

Is your business a limited company, sole proprietorship or a partnership? Who owns the business; shares, percentage split, and how much did they pay or spend for that ownership?

i **Read**
Chapter 4, Business Structure

◎ **Action**
Decide on your structure, take the appropriate actions as outlined in chapter 4 and write the information in this part of your plan.

■ **Example**
KATIE'S NAILS will be the trading name of Katie's Nails Limited. Katie's Nails Limited has one company director and 2 shareholders. The 100 shares are distributed as follows:-

80% - Katie Smith, Managing Director or Company Execute Officer
20% - Steve Smith, Company Secretary

Please note, this is just an example; company secretaries and MD's or CEO's do not necessarily have to be shareholders.

Business Description

A summarised description of your business or business idea is all that is needed at this stage of the plan. The example below will give you an idea of what's needed here.

◎ **Action**
Write down a brief description of what the business does and why.

■ **Example**

KATIE'S NAILS will be a nail salon that provides a comprehensive list of nail, hand and foot treatments to both walk-in and booked clients. The salon will also retail affordable beauty products to salon clients as well as passing trade. The business will address the lack of this service in the residential area of Alberto Square and provide the image conscious women in the area with a friendly and professional nail grooming service.

Business History
(IF YOU ARE ALREADY TRADING)

If your business has already started trading and perhaps you are writing a plan to raise finance for expansion or new equipment, then you should include some business and financial history here.

◎ **Action**

Write a statement about your business so far and add your financial history here. Your accountant would have provided you with yearly business accounts, including the total revenue to date and the breakeven point.

■ **Example**

CHANELLE'S SALON is a nail and tanning salon that has been trading for three years on Alberto Close. It has built an excellent reputation for providing the best spa manicures in E12 and has over 120 regular clients on its records.

The business employs 3 full time and 2 part time beauty therapists and is open six days a week from 10am to 8pm Monday to Saturday, with half day on Wednesday (10am to 3pm). Closing early on a Wednesday provides time for staff meetings, training and team building events.

CHANELLE'S SALON has generated revenues of close to £500,000 in its three years of trading, achieving breakeven at the end of its second year.

---

i See chapter...   ◎ Get it done   ۞ Thinking time   ■ Example   ☺ You can do it!

Revenue

How are you going to make money and how much money are you expecting to make? This is an area that most people starting out don't consider thoroughly. You think to yourself, "I'm opening a beauty salon and that's it. I'll make money from the treatments".

Very bad! You must think creatively about all the possible ways in which your business can generate income. Doing this before starting the business will give you the opportunity to methodically include or introduce these other sources of income in your daily routines and processes; that way you won't be spreading yourself too thin and end up being a *jack of all trades, master of none*!

i Read
Chapter 5, Making Money
Chapter 14, Finances and Accounting, for how to present this information.

◎ Action
List in your plan all the ways in which your business can make money and how much money per year you can expect from these sources. You need to think ahead at least 3 to 5 years.

Services & Products - both use and retail

This section will help you:-

- Plan your treatments.
- Budget for your first stock order.
- Have an idea of how many treatments you expect to get out of the stock.
- And therefore price your treatments correctly.

Remember to think carefully about your market; the customer you are trying to attract and the competition when producing your price list. Avoid over or under pricing and know how best to name the treatments for your audience.

i **Read**
Chapter 5, Making Money
Chapter 13, Marketing

◎ **Action**
At this point in the plan, write two lists; one is your full treatment and retail product list along with prices (basically, your price list), and the other is the list of all the products and items you will need to *use* to give the treatments.

The Management

This section will help you clarify and decide what the different departments are in your organisation and who is responsible for them.

Most of the time in small businesses, the owner is the managing director, head of sales, director of marketing, brand manager, beauty therapist, nail technician, head of finance, operations manager and the whole human resources and customer service department in one!!!

Whatever the case may be, ensure the different roles that are required to run and grow your business efficiently and effectively are clearly defined in this section.

☺ Do not worry if it is just you to start with; just make sure the rest of your plan reflects this fact and you are realistic about your working hours and goals.

◎ **Action**
If the business is a limited company, then list all the directors and company secretary here, otherwise, list all the owners of the business, including:-

- Name
- Age
- Job title
- Job roles
- Proposed yearly salary
- Percentage ownership of the business or company
- CV summary

This will help you define and delegate the different job roles and give any reader (the bank or an investor for example) a clear picture of the experience and skill sets of you and your team.

Staff Requirements

i **Read**
Chapter 7, Staff

◎ **Action**
Write down how many people you will need working in the salon, their salaries and job descriptions and on what basis they will work; full-time, part-time, salaried, self-employed, temporary, agency and so on. How much will you pay them? How do you plan to maintain staff loyalty and keep staff turnover to a minimum?

Salon Premises

In this section talk about your planned premises; its specifications and features.

i **Read**
Chapter 6, Location, Premises & Shop-fit.

◎ **Action**
Write down:-

- Why it is ideal for your business.
- The condition it is in.
- The terms of the lease or contract; how many years, break clauses, termination periods, special conditions or premiums.
- Its dimensions, number of rooms and what will they be used for.
- The yearly rent and ground rent.
- The business rates.
- Any other council bills for say, rubbish disposal.

If you haven't found premises yet, write down what you are ideally looking for, where and what has happened so far in your hunt.

The Shop-fit, Furniture And Decoration

At this point it is really important to have a budget. It is so easy to get carried away with all the gorgeous salon furniture out there, and we all want our salon to be the best and most beautiful... well *stop right there*! Don't overspend at the start; you can always upgrade later when you've made some money. Having said that however, you should still make sure that your salon is decorated in **good taste and at the very least clean, modern and well organised.**

So, decide before you start looking how much you can spend on decorating and furnishing the salon and stick to it.

***i* Read**
Chapter 6, Location, Premises & Shop-fit.

◎ Action
Write a full list of all the shop decoration, furniture and equipment required including lead times, item prices and labour costs.

Suppliers

Decide who your suppliers are going to be. Having created the treatment and product list for your specific market, you should already have an idea as to who your suppliers will be. Make sure that you have thoroughly researched this and sourced the best priced supplier for any specific product. For instance, it may be part of your brand image to use Dermalogica products for facials, but that doesn't mean you must buy your cotton wool and couch roll from them too. There may be another better priced supplier for those items.

Don't be lazy here - this could save your business a lot of money!

i Read
For more on how to source and monitor your salon stock see chapter 8 on Stock.

◎ Action
Write down all your chosen suppliers; including their business names, addresses and telephone numbers.

Opening Hours

◎ Action
Write down your proposed trading hours and anything special about them, like if they are particularly late or early times, then why?

Government Regulations - Licenses, Insurance And Health & Safety

i Read
Chapter 15, Health & Safety, Licensing and Insurance

◎ **Action**

Write down what government regulations affect your business and how you plan to meet those requirements.

Strengths, Weaknesses, Opportunities & Threats - SWOT Analysis

A SWOT analysis is a thorough look at the strengths, weaknesses, opportunities and threats associated with your business.

■ **Example**

Looking at the CHANELLE'S SALON business example, the following could be the SWOT analysis for the business:-

Strengths

- High customer loyalty. Regular customers enjoy the benefits of the loyalty-points scheme offered by the salon with 70% uptake. *(This is a strong indication of a relevant, well planned and executed marketing activity)*

- High staff loyalty. Staff turnover is minimal at 70%; 4 out of 6 members are the same since the salon opened. *(This is a strong indication of good management and an effective recruitment process)*

- Excellent customer service. Having recently performed a customer survey, the business received top marks for customer service, hygiene and treatments. *(This is a strong indication of good management)*

- Shop located on a busy high street. The salon gets a lot of passing traffic and is visited on average by 3 new customers a day. *(This is not really an internal attribute, however it shows good management decision in securing an ideal location for the business)*

- Continued growth in spite of the competition. Even with two other salons within 5 minutes walking distance from Chanelle's Salon, business has shown steady year on year growth. *(This is a strong indication of good management, customer service and marketing)*

Weaknesses

Here, don't leave yourself or your audience wondering what you are doing to solve the issues. Always give information on how you are dealing with the "weakness".

- The business owner, Chanelle, is the salons best and most popular therapist; this means that Chanelle spends most of her time on the shop floor with clients and not enough time managing and marketing the business. This is being addressed with Chanelle slowly moving her clients over to other excellent staff and not taking on any new clients.

- No parking; this is frustrating for some of the clients and may be preventing new customers in cars from popping in. Chanelle is currently in talks with a nearby office building and a local supermarket to see if she can negotiate some parking from them in exchange for staff (or even customer) discounts.

- Some staff members are more versatile than others; this means that certain treatments can only be performed by one staff member. This is being addressed through the Knowledge Sharing Hour Programme held in the salon every Wednesday afternoon; individual staff members do practical demonstrations of their skills while others watch, follow and practice.

- Underutilized first floor; the salon is on the ground floor but the building is on 2 floors. The first floor at the moment is used for storage but there is enough space to add another tanning booth and beauty room.

Opportunities

- The first floor of the salon can be transformed into a tanning booth and treatment room. This will increase sales and reduce the number of clients that are turned away due to lack of space.

- The salon has been approached by a local business to provide their staff with a "beauty half hour" package on a weekly basis. This will increase sales and the customer base.

Threats

- The 10 year lease expires in 2 years and the landlord may not renew it. The salon may have to relocate. However, commercial estate agents have been contacted to start the search for similar and even better premises.

- The salon is located in an area that could soon fall under the congestion charge zone. This is yet to be confirmed; however, half of our clients don't drive to the salon, so it is not clear how much of an effect this will have on business. (PS, you don't have to know everything!)

And so on...

Personal experience

I didn't do this exercise properly before I started my salons and by the time I did, I was already in too deep and way too busy to be creative. This was my fatal error. The biggest strength, weakness, opportunity and threat to my business were the locations. Being in Selfridges&Co and Topshop London was a strength and opportunity for obvious reasons; branding, high footfall, targeted customers and so on. But these locations where also the biggest weakness and threat; the stores could end my contracts and take their floor

space back whenever they wanted to! I always knew that this could potentially be a problem, but I just kept hoping for the best and relying on goodwill. That is just not good enough! I was afraid to think about the consequences and therefore not able to think through and execute solutions. Don't let it happen to you; make sure you do a full SWOT analysis.

◎ **Action**

Think through your SWOT carefully, be objective and open-minded about your business or business idea and really take a good look at what's good and bad about it. Do this now and plan how you will secure and grow the good stuff, and attack and reduce the risks of the bad stuff.

◎ Write down:-

- Strengths - What is really good about your business (internal*)?

- Weaknesses - Where could it grow or do better? What are its limitations (internal*)?

- Opportunities - What opportunities has your business been or could be presented with (external**)?

- Threats - What are the worst-case scenarios for your business and how will you address them (external**)?

* Strengths and weaknesses come from within the business
** Opportunities and threats come from outside the business

You can do a SWOT analysis on your business idea... you don't have to have been trading and have business history to do an analysis.

Section 3 - Marketing

The Marketing Plan (summary)

Marketing is one of the most important things you need to do in business. It is about attracting customers and getting them to spend their money with you again and again. Prepare your marketing plan now.

i **Read**

Please read Chapter 13 on Marketing before attempting this section of the business plan.

Know The Market and Your Market...

The market is the overall beauty industry marketplace. How much money is spent a year on salon visits? How many salons are there in the country? Is the industry healthy and growing, stagnant or in decline. This information can partially help you understand and defend your reasons for wanting a piece of the beauty industry pie... and it's a big pie!

See the Business Link web site, www.businesslink.gov.uk; select Sales and Marketing ⇨ Marketing ⇨ Market Research and Market Reports to get more tips on how to find the relevant data.

Your market is your customer; the person you hope will walk through your salon door. Who is she/he? How old are they? Where do they live? What do they do? Where do they go? How much can they spend? What do they read? What radio stations do they listen to? Do they already get beauty treatments or will you be breaking new ground? Why do they need or want your service?

■ For instance, if you plan to open your salon in Canary Wharf London, you could choose to target the women that work there.

---

 i See chapter...   ◎ Get it done   ♀ Thinking time   ■ Example   ☺ You can do it!

So some of the following would be a way to define your target market:-

Gender	Female
Age	25-45 years old
Income	Employed; £25k - £70k
Transport	Public; buses, trains, tube
Lifestyle	Works Monday to Friday, potentially available for treatments at lunchtime and after work. Not around weekends. She is image conscious; likes to look nice and possibly already has treatments elsewhere.
Publications	Metro, Evening Standard, The Wharf
There are no other similar businesses in the area and as such she needs this service... **_Does she? Is there no competition?_**	

This is the detailed way in which you must research in order to define you target market. Clearly defining your market is vital for any advertising and PR campaigns you design to boost your business. You must not assume or go into any business thinking that as soon as you open the doors, customers will start flocking in out of nowhere! If they do, then that's a fabulous bonus, but if not, you have a plan.

◎ Action

So for the purpose of this part of your business plan, a summary of your marketing plan should include: -

• A statement about the overall industry

• A statement about your market and who you are planning to target and why

• A statement about how you are planning on targeting your specific market

■ Example

A summarised marketing plan

The beauty service industry in the UK is worth £x millions. The beauty salon sector takes up x% of this market. This x% includes hair, nails and beauty treatments with brands such as Toni&Guy and Nails Inc amongst the better known, however there are no major market share leaders.

Our company, Better Beauty aim to meet the quick grooming needs of the following target market:-

Gender	Female
Age	25-45 years old
Income	Employed; £25k - £70k
Transport	Public; buses, trains, tube
Lifestyle	Works Monday to Friday, potentially available for treatments at lunchtime and after work. Not around weekends. She is image conscious; likes to look nice and possibly already has treatments elsewhere.
Publications	Metro, Evening Standard, The Wharf

From our research of 100 women in the x area, we have concluded that there is a gap in the market for providing x services.

We plan to reach and attract this particular audience initially through the following specific marketing activities:-

Here bullet point the ways in which you will do this.

The Brand

What is a brand? Well, without going into too much detail, because there are books and books on this subject; a brand is **everything about the way a business looks and presents itself to the market**. This includes the logo, furniture, uniforms, company colours, the product and treatment list, the customer service style and so on. What is your brand? Whatever you choose, your brand must have a personality that appeals to the market you are trying to target.

i Read
Chapter 13, Marketing

◎ Action
In this part, write down what your brand is or will be.

To help you, look at other brands that you know, and think about what they mean to you, who are they trying to appeal to, what message are they sending out? Then notice how all their adverts or their colours or their images are in-line with that message. (Have a look at The Cowshed, Bliss, Crabtree & Evelyn, Creative Nails, MAC makeup, Miss Sixty, Donna Karen, DKNY; also look at your competitors or other smaller, local businesses and decide what message they are trying to relay).

Doing this exercise will help you with your marketing plan and make sure that whatever actions or direction your business takes, it should remain true to its brand.

Uniqueness

What is your USP – Unique Selling Point?
What makes you different from your competitors? Is it the products that you use? Maybe it's your methods? Or who you are and your reputation? Or your location and the way you offer the service?

◎ Action
Write down your USP.

Customer Loyalty

There are many ways to try and increase customer loyalty; for instance running a loyalty-points scheme, offering special discounts, providing excellent customer service, high quality, well priced treatments and so on. Think creatively and be open-minded about what your methods will be.

◎ Action
Write down what methods you will use to facilitate customer loyalty and how effective you expect them to be.

Competitor Analysis

Know your competition! Where are they, who are they, what are they doing, how much are they charging, how good are they? Try them out. Understand what you are up against; make sure that you have something unique about your offering and keep your standards high.

◎ Action
Create a table of all your competitors. List their names, their offering (i.e. nail bar + tanning shop, beauty salon + hairdressers, etc), their pricelist and their location. Finally list what you are doing or going to do better or different from them.

Personal experience

I'll never forget seeing Marcia Kilgor, founder of Bliss, quietly checking out Nail Haven in Selfridges London around the time they were launching their first UK salon. I was honoured!

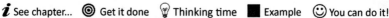

i See chapter...   ◎ Get it done   💡 Thinking time   ■ Example   ☺ You can do it!

The Marketing Budget And Targets

i **Read**
Chapter 13, Marketing

◎ **Action**
Write here approximately how much money you plan to set aside for marketing the business and to what end, meaning, what tangible return are you expecting from this spend.

Schedule of Planned Promotional And Advertising Activities

Having identified your target audience you will be in a better position to understand the types of promotional and advertising activities that should trigger your potential customers' interest in your business.

◎ **Action**
Do the research necessary to evaluate the best places to advertise and the best ways in which to promote the new salon. List your findings along side your schedule of activities and the cost of each activity.

The Future

Where is your business going? Are you planning a national expansion programme? Do you hope to develop your own "secret ingredient" treatment? How will your business cope in changing times? What if your treatments are no longer in fashion? Do you have a plan for the future?

Try to stay ahead in your industry. Keep up to date with the latest trends, products and treatments. Stay in touch with your market. Is it changing? For example, are women no longer attracted to the jobs in Canary Wharf and as such there are now more men in the area; what effect will this have on your salon? How will you adapt?

◎ **Action**
Think about the future and what/where you would like your business to be and how you're going to get there. Write these plans here.

That's the end of Sections 2 and 3 of the business plan...

You have addressed and outlined the basics of your business; who it belongs to, what it does, how it makes money, who runs it, who it's for, where it's going and how it's getting there!

Excellent!

Section 4
Description of Financing

This section is especially important for budgeting and making it clear to any investor or financier how much you need, how you are going to spend the money and what you're offering for the backing.

Proposed Financing – How Much Do You Need And What Are You Offering In Return?

In this section you outline how much money you need to start the business – the **Capital Expenditure**; and out of that how much you are requesting from the bank or investor.

I cannot tell you how much money you need to start your business; that is all subject to so many factors and the choices you make regarding rent, décor, products, wages and so on, but in *i* chapter 14, I go over all the costs that you will definitely incur opening and running a salon; as you do your research, you can add the actual amounts.

i **Read**
Chapter 14, Finances and Accounting

◎ **Action**
Write here your total start-up costs (capital expenditure). Then how much money you have or plan to put in, any other sources of funding (like a bank loan or your friends and family investing some money) and finally how much you are requesting.

■ **Example**
Total planned start-up costs (Capital Expenditure) = £70,000.00
Current available funds = £20,000.00 this is a mixture of equity and

debt financing (see table below)
Funds requested = £50,000.00 for 30% equity ownership

Miss Founder (Investor & Manager)	£5,000
Bank Loan	£5,000
Miss Friend Family (Investor)	£10,000
Funds requested (Investor)	£50,000
Total capital required	**£70,000**

Ownership And Return On Investment (ROI)

In this section you are trying to show who owns what before the new investment, who will own what after the new investment and finally what the returns on investment will be, i.e., how much money will everybody make from their ownership.

In a Sole Proprietorship this is very straight forward and is up to you, the owner; how you want to split the profits with your investors. In a Limited Company structure, how shares are divided can have various tax implications, so you are strongly advised to discuss any distribution of shares with your accountant first.

i **Read**
Chapter 14 before you complete the ROI

◎ **Action**
Start by listing in table format who all the business owners or shareholders are, and what percentage ownership they currently have. Then in another table, list what will happen to the ownership when/if a new investor comes on board. Will the percentages of the original shareholders be diluted or will one person "sell" some of their shares for the investment?

Finally outline what the ROI will be. For this you will need to have

---

prepared your Profit & Loss forecasts (P&L) and calculated your market share. The ROI can be a straightforward calculation based on the profits of the business but if you are planning on selling your business after a period of trading the ROI will be based on the value of the business which could be much higher than its profits; this is subject to many factors.

■ Example
Before new investment:-

Miss Founder	90%
Miss Friend Family	10%

After new investment:-
If offering the new investor 30% for their £50,000.00 investment and diluting the current ownership, then you would end up with the following split:-

Miss Founder	63%
Miss Friend Family	7%
Miss New Investor	30%

If you plan to sell your shares and not affect Miss Friend Family's ownership, then you could end up with the following split:-

Miss Founder	60%
Miss Friend Family	10%
Miss New Investor	30%

■ Example - Return on investment - ROI
In 5 years time we plan to have acquired 2% of the Manchester Beauty Salon market. This market is worth £100 million; therefore our share is equivalent to £2 million turnover, as demonstrated in the businesses/company's 5 year Profit & Loss forecast.

Profits expected at the end of year 5 are £400,000.00 after reinvestments into the business, and will be distributed according to ownership.

Therefore the expected profit distribution:-

Miss Founder	£252,000	63%
Miss Friend Family	£28,000	7%
Miss New Investor	£120,000	30%

Therefore ROI for new investor, investing £50,000.00 and receiving £120,000.00 in 5 years is 240%.

Please remember...

The above is just an example; the calculations are correct but all the figures are fictional. If your expected turnover is much less or much more, or you have many more investors, or you plan to sell the business, the layout for this section remains the same and ultimately has the same purpose in your business plan.

Use Of Proceeds – How Are You Going To Spend The Start-Up/Capital Money?

◎ **Action**
Present this in a table format also.

■ **Example**

Expenses	When	Amount
Premises deposit and rent	January	£6,000
Web site	February	£700
Printing	February	£300
Shop-fit	January	£15,000

Expenses	When	Amount
Equipment	January	£4,000
Advertising	Jan-July	£10,000
Stock	January	£5,000
PR Agency	Feb-May	£9,000
3 months salaries	Feb-April	£12,000
Professional fees	Jan-Dec	£3,000
Miscellaneous		£5,000
Total		£70,000

This will give your investor a quick view of how the money will be spent.

Reporting

How are you going to keep your investors and yourself up-to-date and informed about the progress of the business? What reports will you produce? How often?

Usually for investors or silent partners, reporting every 6 months to a year is expected. But for yourself or/and your manager(s) daily, weekly, monthly and yearly reports will be needed. I would even go as far as to suggest you get hourly reports on your business! Relevant and regular reports help you understand your staffs' productivity, what areas of the salon make the most money, what areas need attention and how well your business is doing overall.

◎ Action
In this part of the plan, for investors and lenders, write down what reports you will produce and how often. Generally speaking, the most relevant reports for investors and lenders are the Profit & Loss, Balance Sheet and Cash Flow statements prepared every 6 to 12 months.

Investor Involvement

Investors can be silent partners, i.e. have no role in the running of the business; or they could be heavily involved and have the power to execute tasks; or they could just be advisors and have no decision making power at all.

◎ Action
State here what the investor's involvement will be.

■ Example
You have 3 investors; Miss Friend Family may actually be in charge of the businesses finances because she is a trained accountant and for her skill and £5,000.00 investment you have offered her 7% of the business and an annual salary of £15,000. So she is a decision maker and has the power to execute tasks. Her involvement in the business should be clearly outlined in your partnership agreement and she should have an employment contract.

Miss New Investor may know a lot about product launches and you asked her to invest in your business because she can also advise on how best to launch your own brand of skincare. So her role in the business is as an advisor, with no execution responsibilities. This must be outlined in your partnership agreement.

Fees Paid

This section is referring to any fees incurred while securing investment, such as legal fees and who will pay them. Decide if you will be paying the fees for both parties or just your own fees or if the investor will pay the fees for both parties.

◎ Action
State here who is paying for what.

Important...

It is vital that you get legal and financial advice that is in your best interest during any investor transactions. Have your own solicitor and accountant check what agreements are being drawn up by your investors professional team; or better still have your team draw up the documents first (this may be more costly to you though).

That's the end of Section 4 of the business plan...

You have now stated how much money you need, how you will spend it, what you are giving in return and the terms of your relationship.

Great!

Section 5 Analysis of Finance, Financial Statements and Projections

This section is a thorough breakdown of all your financial projections. How much money will the business make, how have you come to those amounts, how will the business spend its money on an ongoing basis? All of these questions should be answered in this section.

Cash Flow Forecast

i Read
Chapter 14 for what Cash Flow means and how to prepare and present a Cash Flow forecast.

◎ Action
Insert in here your 3 to 5 year Cash Flow forecast

Profit & Loss Forecast

i Read
Chapter 14 for what Profit & Loss means and how to prepare and present a Cash Flow forecast.

◎ Action
Insert in here your 3 to 5 year P&L forecast

---

i See chapter...   ◎ Get it done   💡 Thinking time   ■ Example   ☺ You can do it!

Assumptions And Other Calculations

This section gives the reader an understanding of how you came about your revenue and cost estimates. Here you should clearly outline all your calculations along with any assumptions you have made.

For an ■ example, in *i* chapter 14, I show how I calculated the sales forecast for a particular salon.

◎ **Action**
Insert here what assumptions and calculations you made when preparing your forecasts.

That's the end of Section 5 of the business plan...

You have now thoroughly described the businesses finances and shown that it is a viable business.

Fantastic!

Section 6
Operations and Processes

The business operations and processes describe how the salon is/ will be run on a day to day basis. How is stock ordered, hygiene maintained and shop repairs handled? What about hiring staff, training and paying bills? How about where the customer puts their wet coat and umbrella in a busy nail bar or hairdressers?

Knowing the answers to these questions and having clear guidelines as to how your salon functions will make for a much smoother running ship. Customers will be happier, staff will feel looked after and you will be a lot saner! So it is very important that you plan how you will run and manage your shop.

This part of the business plan can get very detailed and is really only useful to you and your team. So unless specifically asked by your potential investor or bank manager, ◎ leave Section 6 out of the plan.

To help you create your salon processes and manage operations, read the following *i* chapters 7 - 12

If however you are requested to add Section 6 to your plan, then from experience, the following headings are the most popular and relevant:-

Recruitment Process

This section should cover every aspect of hiring, paying and firing staff in your salon.

i **Read**
Chapter 7, Staff

i See chapter... ◎ Get it done 💡 Thinking time ■ Example ☺ You can do it!

◎ **Action**

Outline here how you plan to recruit staff for your salon, including where you will advertise for them, what the selection process and criteria will be, how often and by what means they will be paid and so on.

Training Programme

Will you have a formal training programme for your staff? Or may be you will create a weekly skill-sharing session between staff. Will staff be required to pay for any training they receive during their employment? These are the types of questions that need to be answered in this section.

i **Read**

Chapter 7, Staff

◎ **Action**

Describe what methods you will use to keep staff performing great treatments and knowledgeable about the products they use and sell. Also describe how you will monitor performance and provide opportunities for performance improvement.

Stock Order And Control

How often will you order stock and how will its usage be monitored? Poor stock management is a costly business; from theft to misuse on the shop floor, it is therefore important to create robust methods for stock management.

i **Read**

Chapter 8, Stock

◎ **Action**

Outline your stock management plans here.

Quality Control

Quality control covers everything from monitoring how well treatments are performed to how well tools are cleaned and disinfected in the salon. From how well customers are greeted and treated to whether staff are well informed on the salons latest offers.

Quality can be monitored in a variety of ways, for example through mystery shoppers, regular salon inspections and staff performance reviews.

i **Read**
Chapter 7, Staff
Chapter 10, The Reception Area
Chapter 11, On-Going Management
Chapter 12, Customer Service

◎ **Action**
Outline what methods you will use to monitor and maintain quality in your salon.

Customer Complaints

Every salon should have a customer complaints policy. This should clearly outline, to all staff, the company's preferred method of handling a complaint. Empowering staff to deal with a dissatisfied customer quickly and in the correct manner can sometimes save the day!

i **Read**
Chapter 12, Customer Service

◎ **Action**
Describe your customer complaints policy here, including the salons refund policy.

Salon Law And Order

Here, I am referring to the general management of staff and customers. Staff rotas, the appointment system, clients record cards, till and cash management, lateness, etc. These should all be thought through and management processes put in place.

i **Read**
Chapter 7, Staff
Chapter 8, Stock
Chapter 10, The Reception Area
Chapter 11, On-Going Management
Chapter 12, Customer Service

◎ **Action**
Describe how you will manage all the other salon operations here.

That's the end of Section 6 of the business plan...

You have addressed and outlined how your business is or will be run and managed on a day-to-day basis.

Again, Excellent!

Summary

This section is for a quick recap of the business plan and serves as a positive reminder of all the aspects of the business that are important to an investor.

■ **Example**

Better Beauty will be a unique salon in the heart of Manchester, offering the local 25 to 45 year old female the complete grooming service in a comfortable, friendly and sophisticated environment. We have access to excellent therapists and the salon manager/owner has 10 years experience in the industry. We intend to generate income through a range of services and plan to partner with beauty exhibitors to provide a comprehensive list of treatments, retail the full range of aftercare products and sell advertising space. The business expects to breakeven by the middle of year 2 and reach a sustainable turnover of £2 million per annum by year 5, with a gross profit margin of 19%. This is a unique opportunity for any investor as the market in this area is untapped.

Points To Note From Above Summary

The above statement is attractive to an investor for the following reasons:-

* Unique salon
* Access to excellent therapists
* Salon manager/owner has 10 years experience in the industry
* Breakeven by the middle of year 2 (18 months)
* Sustainable turnover of £2 million
* Gross profit margin of 19%
* The market in this area is untapped

Of course your business plan must be able to back up all your statements!

---

 i See chapter... ◎ Get it done ♀ Thinking time ■ Example ☺ You can do it!

That's the end of the business plan...

Congratulations for working so hard on this! I am sure that you now see your business in a totally different light and have a clear plan of action and vision for the future.

Well done and good luck!

Chapter 4
Business Structure

The big question...

Are you going to trade as a sole proprietor, a partnership or a limited company and what are the differences?

In this chapter, I will outline your legal responsibilities as well as any actions that you will be required to take under each structure; adding wherever possible my own little extras! It is then for you to decide what suits your particular circumstances best.

Whatever choice you make, you will need a good accountant and solicitor (lawyer) at this stage. See *i* chapter 16 on Professional Services, to help you find and choose professionals for your business.

SOLE PROPRIETOR / SOLE TRADER

What Is?

A Sole Proprietorship is the simplest way to run a business. Simple in that you only answer to yourself and the taxman! It is not a company but a way for you to do business under a trading name. So for instance if you are Josephine Blog and you name your business Better Beauty then as a Sole Trader you will be Josephine Blog T/A Better Beauty (T/A means Trading As). This means that any bills, loans or credit that Better Beauty has, are actually bills, loans and credit to you. And any profit made by the business is yours (less your personal tax).

Please note; before choosing a trading name check that it is not already in use; for more on this see chapter 13 on Marketing; choosing a business name and logo. Also remember that a trading name can be your actual name.

Why Not?

If your business needs a lot of debt financing or is likely to incur high bills with creditors, then being a sole trader may not be the best option for you. This is because if anything happens to the business you will be fully liable for all of its debts!

Tax

A sole trader's employment status is 'Self-Employed'. As a self-employed person you will need to register yourself for tax within 3 months of becoming self-employed. You will also be required to pay your personal tax bill at the end of each tax year. This involves you (or your accountant) completing a yearly Self-Assessment Tax Return from which your tax liabilities will be calculated. The tax year runs from the 6th April to the 5th April.

Other

You should open a business bank account to help you keep your personal finances separate from the business ones. You must keep all your bank statements, receipts and cash transaction records to prove your businesses income and expenses; see more on this in *i* chapters 11 and 14.

More information for UK readers
Business Link
www.businesslink.gov.uk (see - Starting up)

HM Revenue and Customs (HMRC)
Newly Self-Employed Helpline 08459 15 45 15

i See chapter... ◎ Get it done ♀ Thinking time ■ Example ☺ You can do it!

PARTNERSHIP

What Is?

A partnership in a business has the same structure as the sole trader except that the business is shared between the partners. How it is shared is up to you; it can be 50:50 or 70:30 or any other split you agree on. The split could represent the work responsibilities or the profit share or the debt share or a combination of any or all of the above; it's up to you and your partner(s).

You can and should create a trading name; for example, Josephine Blog and Michael Blog T/A Blog and Blog Salons. Again check the availability of the name.

Tax

In terms of tax, the partnership will be seen as one entity and each partner as an individual. This means that yearly, you (or your accountant) will need to complete a Partnership Tax Return for the business as a whole, as well as individual Self-Assessment Tax Returns for each partner.

The Partnership Agreement

It is absolutely vital that you and your partners take the time to put the terms of your partnership in writing. I know in the beginning when everyone is enthusiastic, excited and happy this all seems unnecessary, but I cannot stress enough how necessary a well thought-out written agreement is.

Having a written partnership agreement is very important!

How The Road Ahead Can Change!

- Enthusiasm, excitement and happiness are not necessarily feelings that last once the business has started and the realities of the hard work and commitment required to succeed set in! "I can't come into the shop today because I need to so something else"! "I haven't finished that task yet because I had another commitment"!

- Once the business starts to generate income, a person's attitude towards the partnership can change. "I did most of the work"! "There would be no business if not for me"! "Why are you getting an equal share when you haven't put in as much effort"?!

- Trust is best left out of business; rely on a written agreement instead! Of course you want to be in business with someone trustworthy but where money is involved, who knows what issues may arise.

Think of a partnership as a long-term commitment to another person, with whom you are going to be sharing your hopes, dreams, ambitions and money. Try and choose partners that you know well; have a good idea of their character and importantly their actual skill set.

Your written agreement should (at least) include the following:-

- The partners; their names, addresses and contact details;
- Initial cash and asset investments;
- A list of each individual's relevant experience and expertise;
- Each partners job title and completely defined job roles for before and after the business launches;
- The percentage ownership split; will this split relate to debts?

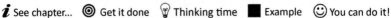

- A statement about how decisions will be made;
- A statement about how and when profits will be distributed;
- Salaries, if appropriate;
- A statement about how disputes will be resolved;
- Signed declarations

This is not an exhaustive list; if you are unsure you should have a solicitor read through the agreement.

Remember, agreements can be flexible; you could state that due to certain variable factors the written agreement will be reviewed every 6 months to ensure its continued relevance.

Also partners don't have to have equal share of the business or take on equal responsibilities; the ownership can be divided to suit everyone's input. You could have a sleeping partner; someone who doesn't manage or make any decisions about the business but invests cash in return for profits.

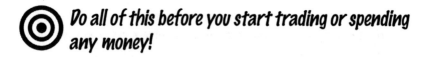 **Do all of this before you start trading or spending any money!**

A LIMITED COMPANY

What Is?

There are a few different types of companies but the most common company structure is a Private Limited Company (Ltd.).

The most important thing to understand about a company is that it is its own entity and you as the managing director/CEO work for it. All the money the business earns belongs to the company first and then, as a director and therefore employee you are paid a salary or dividends if profit is made.

When a person says they own their own company, what they mean is that they are the main or only shareholder of the company's shares. A managing director or CEO of a company is an officer of the company whose job is to run the business in such a way as to provide the best returns possible for the company's shareholders, i.e., the owners! The shareholders are the owners of a company; not the directors. Of course, directors can also be shareholders, but they can be sacked and replaced by the majority shareholders.

For example
Say 100% of a company has 100 shares.
You own 45% = 45 shares (with voting rights)
X owns 20% = 20 shares (with voting rights)
Y owns 35% = 35 shares (with voting rights)

In this example you are a shareholder as well as the managing director of the company. As the MD you are taking on the responsibility of running the business, making decisions that are in the best interests of the company and looking after all the other shareholders.

Say after sometime the other two shareholders decide that they are unhappy with the way you are running the salon; maybe they feel you are not working hard enough or don't have the right skills to do the best job. Because their combined ownership of the company outweighs your own; 55% to 45%, they have the power to sack and replace you! No one, however, can take your shares away from you; you will still own 45% of the business.

Tip...

If you want ultimate control of your company you will need to ensure

that you always hold the majority shares.

What If You Own All The Company Shares?

Then you will only have to look after yourself! So how is this different from being a sole trader? Well, as previously mentioned, if something goes wrong with the business as a sole trader, you have no shield to protect you from any debts; all business debts are your debts. So in the worst-case scenario you will suffer a bad credit rating, loss of all assets and/or bankruptcy! If however, something goes wrong in a limited company you are shielded from the debts (as long as you didn't personally guarantee them) as all business debts are the company's debts. This may sound great but the reality is that due to the nature of this "shield" your conduct as a director of the company will be completely scrutinised and investigated to ensure that your actions did not lead to this failure and more importantly, that you did not ignore the signs of imminent closure and continue to trade incurring further debts when there was no way to pay! The consequences of this can include liquidation of the company, loss of the trading name, disqualification as a company director for anything from 3 to 15 years depending on how badly you behaved and more!

Don't dwell on this...

Please don't dwell on this doom and gloom information. I have only added this in to make you as aware as possible of the essence behind the different business structures; not to put you off business! Ideally you will do a great job of running your business and there will be no need to look at bad endings!

So Why Trade As A Limited Company?

- As mentioned above you will not be liable, unless personally guaranteed, for any of the businesses debts. This is especially useful if your business requires a lot of investment or credit, or is planning a relatively aggressive expansion programme.

- Generally investors and other companies like to deal with businesses that are required to be public about their accounts and structure. Every year a company's accounts must be submitted to Companies House. These accounts are then made available for public inspection. In a partnership or sole proprietorship, you don't have to share your business dealings with anyone other than HMRC and your business partners.

- There can be substantial tax benefits to trading as a limited company. Ask your accountant about this.

Important...

Again as a company director, you a fully responsible for the conduct and financial dealings of the company and all the decisions you make must be in the best interest of the company and not your own. If the company runs into trouble, and is no longer able to pay its bills when they become due, as a director you must immediately take the appropriate actions and seek professional advice from your accountant and solicitor. If you continue to incur debts knowing full well that the company is unable to meet those debts then you are acting irresponsibly as an officer of that company and could face harsh consequences as previously mentioned.

More information for UK readers
There is a lot more information about companies and directors responsibilities on the Companies House web site or you can telephone them, ask questions and receive their information by post.

Companies House - www.companieshouse.gov.uk

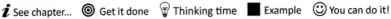

Company Registration

To start a company you must register it with Companies House. You will need a minimum of 2 company officers - a director and a company secretary.

There are 2 forms and 2 documents to complete, these are:-

Form 10
This form gives details of the first director(s), secretary and the intended address of the registered office;

Form 12
This form is a statutory declaration of compliance with all the legal requirements relating to the incorporation of a company;

Articles of Association
This document sets out the rules for the running of the company's internal affairs;

Memorandum of Association
This document sets out the company's name, registered office and what it will do.

You can download forms 10 and 12 for free from the Companies House web site or telephone them on 08703 33 36 36. The Articles and Memorandum of Association need to be purchased from a legal stationers like OYEZ Straker; these documents are around £11 each. See www.oyezformslink.co.uk

Form 12 and the Arts and Mems documents will need to be signed in front of a solicitor, commissioner for oaths, a notary public or a justice of the peace. Solicitors usually charge £5 to £10 for this service.

After you have completed all 4 forms post them to Companies House for registration. Companies House charge £20 for standard registration.

All together, registering a company on your own costs around £50, however, for a £100, companies like OYEZ Straker can register your company for you and save you all the hassle. A solicitor or accountant can also help you register your company.

MAKING YOUR DECISION

There is a lot of information out there and below are the best places to get help (UK readers):-

Business Link

www.businesslink.gov.uk

Business Link offer practical advice for business. They have a great Interactive Tool to help you decide on what structure is best for you. They also have real business people telling their stories of how they made the decision. Visit the Business Link web site.

Companies House

www.companieshouse.gov.uk
08703 33 36 36

Their main functions are to:-
- Incorporate and dissolve limited companies;
- Examine and store company information delivered under the Companies Act and related legislation; and
- Make this information available to the public.

Companies House hold Seminars in their Cardiff and Glasgow offices for **Newly Appointed Directors & Secretaries**, to help keep companies on the right side of the law. Call or visit their web site for more details and available dates.

Inland Revenue Business Support

www.hmrc.gov.uk/businesses
08459 15 45 15

You can arrange an appointment with the Business Support Team to get practical advice on tax matters that will affect you. Or read and download the Beginners Guide to Working for Yourself or Starting a Business.

Take the time to read and think about your business and its future when deciding on the best structure for you.

Chapter 5
MAKING MONEY

That's the name of the game!

Making money is what it's all about!

Yes, there's the stuff about working for yourself and being your own boss... proving to yourself that you can do it and having that sense of achievement... you may also have the goal to provide the best facials this side of the Atlantic... BUT, if no one is paying you for it, you won't last long! So in the very end, making money is what it's all about and you will know that you have been successful when you can pay all your bills and have real financial freedom while your business continues to grow.

 Start thinking about the different ways in which your business can and will generate income...

MONEY MAKER NUMBER 1 - TREATMENTS

Obviously, this is one of your main two core money generators; the other being product retail. Are you planning to offer all the treatments you can? Are there any treatments that can be offered with minimum work? Is there a more exciting and up-to-date way of packaging your treatment list?

■ **Example**

Treatments that don't require a therapists time:-
* Self service tanning booths
* Spa Jet Foot Massage with music, tea and biscuits
* Acrylic nail soak-off with audio story
* Half hour power nap with dolphin music (with 5 min head rub to get the client started)

Treatments that can be in addition to a main:-
- Hand massage with an express manicure
- Shoulder and neck rub with deep cleansing facial

Treatment packages based on time:-
- "The Quick Groom™" 30 minutes – manicure, blow-dry, toe polish £45

- "Relax in the City™" 30 minutes - Shoulder and neck rub, foot massage, eye pack £25

- "Hello, I'm back!™" 1 hour – Eyebrow & Eyelash tint or threading, express manicure & pedicure and wash & blow dry £55

And so on...

All of these things depend on your location and your market so have a really good think about what you can offer your clients to boost your sales.

Treatment List And Durations

Having researched different salons and spoken to many technicians, I have compiled a list of the most popular treatments and how long they should take to do on average.

You must create your own list and maybe call your treatments nice names if that is part of your brand image and marketing plan.

You could take the straight forward approach and name your treatments as they are, see examples at:-

- The Face & Form Salon; see www.faceandform.co.uk
- The Only You Hair & Beauty Salon; see www.onlyyousalon.co.uk

Or you could be creative and name your treatments something fun,

see ■ examples at:-

- The Chocolate Pink Salon; see www.choccypink.com
- The Bliss Salon; see www.blissworld.com

Again base this decision on your market.

Remember that your treatment list and how long each one takes to do is entirely up to you, but bear in mind that you are trying to achieve customer satisfaction and a profit! So creating a fancy 2 hour back rub with gold oil may be nice, but does your customer actually want it, do they even have the time for it and can you charge enough for the time, effort, space and gold you have put into it!?

Nails

Shape and paint	15 minutes
Basic manicures	20 minutes
Deluxe/complete manicures	1 hour
Basic pedicures	30 minutes
Deluxe/complete pedicures	1 hour
Nail Extensions	1 hour 15 minutes
In-fills	1 hour
Nail Art	Various
Buff and Polish	15 minutes

Hair

Consultation	10 minutes
Shampoo and finish	45 minutes
Cut, shampoo and finish	1 hour 15 minutes
Blow dry or GHD only	15 – 40 minutes
Highlights/Lowlights	1 hour plus
Full head colour change	1 hour plus

Root colour retouch	50 minutes
Whole head retouch	1 hour plus
Hair straightening/Relaxer	1 hour 30 minutes
Permanent Curl	1 hour 30 minutes
Afro relaxer retouch	1 hour
Shampoo/Condition	15 minutes
Deep conditioning treatments	20 minutes
Trim	10 minutes
Redesign haircut	45minutes
Hair Extensions	Various
Braids	Various

Facials

Basic facials	30 - 45 minutes
Specialist facials	1 hour
Eye treatments	Various

Body

Scrubs	1 – 1 hour 30 minutes
Applied tans	1 hour
Spray tans	15 minutes
Wraps	1 hour plus
Baths	1 hour

Massage

Back	Various
Head	Various
Neck and shoulders	Various
Full body	Various
Lower body	Various
Upper body	Various
Specialist massages	Various

Makeup

Consultation	15 minutes
Full face	30 minutes
Restyle	45 minutes
Lessons	1 hour

Waxing

Eyebrow	10 minutes
Full leg	30 minutes
Half leg	15 minutes
Under arm	10 minutes
Bikini	10 minutes
Brazilian	25 minutes
Arms	20 minutes
Back	20 minutes
Chest	15 minutes
Lip	5 minutes
Chin	5 minutes

Cosmetic Enhancements

Teeth whitening	1 hour
Eyebrow tinting	15 minutes
Eyelash tinting	15 minutes
Eyelash extensions	30 minutes
Threading	10 minutes
Skin rejuvenation treatments	30 minutes plus
Electrolysis	Various
Botox®	1 hour
Semi-permanent makeup	1 hour plus

Pricing Treatments

How do I decide what to charge my customers? This is a big question! In short, I suggest that you calculate the total cost of the treatment and add your profits on top; bearing in mind your market and your competitors prices.

I would do the following:-
Firstly, check out the competition; study their price-lists, note their locations and the quality of their services. This is just for guidance as you don't want to price yourself out of the market or be too cheap either. Remember, don't copy your competition; you must aim to be

unique in some way.

Next, calculate how much you would have to spend in order to give a treatment. How much are the business' **Direct Costs** per treatment; wages, rent and stock?

Also, estimate how many treatments you can do in a day from one **Money-Making-Station**, i.e., nail station, treatment room, tanning booth, hair station, etc. How busy do you really think you will be?

Then go on to estimate the business' **Indirect Costs** per treatment; banking charges, professional fees, advertising, your wages, etc.

Finally, add on your ideal profit margin and if possible an amount to reinvest in the business.

Here Is An Example Of The Calculations...

In this example we will look at both Direct and Indirect costs. Direct costs are costs that can be directly traced to the product or service.

 For example, the shop rent is a direct cost of a manicure; if you don't have premises then you can't do the manicure. Indirect costs are costs that cannot be traced directly to the product or service and are therefore overheads. For example, the cost of printing your price lists is an indirect cost or overhead of the manicure; you can still do a manicure without a price list.

Also see *i* chapter 14, Finance and Accounting for more on this.

Pricing every treatment is advisable; this will help you with planning discounts, special offers and creating packages. So when you decide to give 10% off or more you will know what your profit or loss will be!

Don't panic if you are adverse to numbers, you can purchase a **Treatment and Product Pricing Calculator** from www. misssalonbusiness.com for £24.99.

■ **Example**

Information you need to have; example figures...

Shop Rent	£12,000.00 per year
Staff wages	£7.00 per hour
Employer NIC	11% (UK National Insurance Contributions)
Trading hours	9 hours per day / 6 days per week
VAT (UK tax on goods)	17.5%

The salon has 10 Money-Making-Stations (**MMS**); these are work areas like a treatment room, nail station, tan booth or hair station.

So to determine the Direct Costs of a 1 hour facial you would do the following calculations:-

Rent per station per hour
£12,000 rent divided by 10 MMS = £1,200 rent per station per year
So each station needs to make £1,200 per year to cover the rent.
(12,000 ÷ 10 = £1,200 per station per year)

The salon is open 6 days a week so with 52 weeks in a year we have 312 working days.
(52 x 6 = 312 working days per year)

312 working days times 9 hours a day = 2,808 opening hours in a year (312 x 9 = 2,808 opening hours per year)

Therefore, in 1 hour, 1 station needs to make
1,200 (£) divided by 2,808 (hours) = 42p per hour to cover the rent.
(£1,200 ÷ 2,808 = £0.42 rent per station per hour)

Wages per employee per hour
Staff member is paid £7.00 per hour in this example.
Employer's national insurance contributions are around 11%.

So you will pay an extra 77 pence per hour for that staff member.
Therefore, the wages cost for that 1 hour facial is £7.77.
(£7.00 x 11% = £0.77 + £7.00 = £7.77 per hour)

Stock used per facial
This can be a bit detailed but here goes!
We want to list all the products and items we will use in the facial,
how much we pay for each, how many facials we can get out of each
bottle and therefore the product cost for each facial...

So in this example,
£20 Face cleanser 100ml = 20 facials = £1 per facial
£20 Exfoliating cream 100ml = 20 facials = £1 per facial
£20 Face Mask 100ml = 20 facials = £1 per facial
£20 Moisturiser 100ml = 20 facials = £1 per facial
£10 Cotton Discs Carton = 100 facials = 10 pence per facial
£5 Couch roll = 40 facials = 12.5 pence per facial
Towel laundry at £1 per towel and 1 towel per client = £1 per facial

Therefore the total cost of stock used in this 1 hour facial is:-

£5.23 (including postage & packaging and VAT that you paid when
purchasing the products to use)

Utilities per MMS per hour
Say the electricity bill is £1,200 per year = 42 pence per hour = 4.2
pence per station

(£1,200 ÷ 2,808 trading hours = £0.42 10 MMS = £0.04 electricity
per station per hour)

Say the water bill is £250 per year = negligible

Soooooooo...

The total direct costs of a 1 hour facial in this case are:-

Rent	£0.42
Wages	£7.77
Stock	£5.23
Utilities	£0.04
Total Direct Costs of 1 hour facial	**£13.46**

That's how much the direct costs of a 1 hour facial are.

What about the indirect costs; the accountant, the leaflets, the bank charges, the business rates, the telephone bills, the advertising, the insurance and so on? Remember these costs need to be taken into account as well.

What about your wages and your investors and their returns on investment? What about profit?

The easiest way to calculate the indirect costs on a 1 hour facial is by adding up all the yearly indirect costs (see *i* chapter 14 for a list of indirect costs) and dividing them by 2,808 opening/trading hours in a year and then again by the 10 Money Making Stations (MMS).

So, if my yearly indirect costs are £60,000.00
Then 60,000 divided by 2,808 = £21.37 per hour
£21.37 divided by 10 stations = £2.14 per station per hour
(£60,000 ÷ 2,808 = £21.37 ÷ 10 = £2.14 per station per hour)

Total Indirect Costs of 1 hour facial	**£2.14**

So the real cost of the 1 hour facial is **£13.46 direct + £2.14 indirect = £15.60**

Say you would like to invest £10.00 back into the business per facial and also you would like to make a profit of £15.00 per facial.

You would need to charge your customer:-

Costs	£15.60
Reinvest (for maintenance and growth)	£10.00
Profit (37% of total excluding VAT)	£15.00
Total	£40.60
VAT	£7.11

Therefore the price of facial to the customer is £47.71

Important...

The above calculation is based on all your work stations being busy the entire time the salon is open... this is not very realistic!

What if we look at being busy half the time?

That is 1,404 money making hours.
Remember you are still trading for 2,808 hours a year but only busy half the time...

(2,808 ÷ 2 = 1,404 or 2,808 x 50% = 1,404)

The rent and indirect costs will change per facial to:-

Rent

£1,200 ÷ 1,404 hours = £0.85 per station per hour

Indirect costs

£60,000 ÷ 1,404 hours = £42.74 ÷ 10 stations = £4.27 per station per hour

---

 i See chapter... ◎ Get it done ♀ Thinking time ■ Example ☺ You can do it!

So the new totals are:-

Rent	£0.85
Wages	£7.77
Stock	£5.23
Utilities	£0.04
Indirect costs	£4.27
Reinvest	£10.00
Profit (35% of total excluding VAT)	£15.00
Total	**£43.16**
VAT	£7.55

The new total price of a facial to the customer is £50.71

What if we look at being busy 25% of the time?

That is, 702 money making hours
(2,808 ÷ 4 = 702 or 2,808 x 25% = 702)

Following the same steps as shown above

The new total price of a facial to the customer is £56.75

Remember...

These calculations are based on fictional costs. Make sure your calculations are based on your particular costs.

Ask yourself...
Are these prices realistic for your target market? What are your competitors charging? If they are too expensive, then you will need to look at your

costs and see where you can reduce them. Start with your indirect costs (the overheads) and then with the cost of the stock and how many treatments you get out of one bottle. This is where good stock control will be vital. If you can get 5 more facials out of your products that would significantly reduce the cost of stock on each treatment.

Finally, make your treatments make money for you!

MONEY MAKER NUMBER 2 - PRODUCT RETAIL

This is your second core money generator; but making the most of this revenue stream is not easy.

Common issues that you'll come across are:-

- I'm a beauty therapist not a sales girl
- I don't like selling, I feel like I'm forcing the customer to buy the product
- I tried to sell but she's already got it at home
- I'm trying but nobody wants to spend any money

The list goes on!

Your Business Must Retail...

First things first, know that your business will struggle without retail revenue; the £10 you make from a manicure that takes 20 minutes, you can make from selling a bottle of cuticle oil in 2 minutes. The most successful salon businesses are the ones that sell products as part of their "main course".

☺Decide from the start that, not retailing products is not an option!

---

  i See chapter... ◎ Get it done ♀ Thinking time ■ Example ☺ You can do it!

Mediocre sales is not what you are in business for. If you are not going to take product sales seriously then there is no point opening a salon! OOOooooo, tough talk!

Three Main Ways To Sell...

Selling through the staff and as aftercare

When hiring staff, make sure that they understand that their job role includes selling products. As beauty therapists, nail technicians, receptionists, makeup artists or hairdressers, they know their jobs involve opportunities to encourage clients to use more of the salon's products and services, as such everybody delivering products and services needs to play a part in making clients aware of what is available as well as encouraging them to return to the salon. Staff should understand that selling home maintenance products to their clients is part of good customer service.

Of course, not everyone is a natural sales person and most will need training in this area, but they must be willing to learn and to practise the art of selling until they get it right.

Please see *i* chapter 9 on Retail for tips on how to train your staff to sell!

Selling through visual display; merchandising well

Products need to be displayed well and in a coherent manner. Try to always have fully stocked shelves. Keep similar products together and try to keep the "frilly" stuff to a minimum; by frilly I mean decoration or display only items. Too many frills around products make it a "no go/don't touch" area for customers. Think Boots, Superdrug and Sainsbury's when merchandising. Keep your products and offers updated and make sure your displays are fresh and dust free!

Selling through easy-reach products and testers

Wouldn't it be great if people just walked in off the street, picked up an item and paid for it at reception? What an income booster.

Make your waiting area a money making station as well! Have all your retail at easy reach with clearly labelled testers for each of the items. Put a sign in your window or on your actual signage telling people that you sell professional beauty brands.

Pricing Product

Thankfully this is not as complicated as treatments! However you may choose to motivate your staff to sell by paying a commission, this will need to be factored into your pricing.

Most suppliers will give you a **Recommended Retail Price (RRP)** for their products; these prices may or may not be good for your particular business circumstances so make sure you know your direct costs first. Please note - some suppliers and manufacturers are not flexible on their RRP's.

Working Out Whether The RRP Is Good For Your Business...

To do this you will need to consider:-

- The price you paid for it including postage & packaging and VAT (especially if you are not VAT registered, which means you won't get it back! See *i* chapter 14)
- Any commission you may be paying your staff to sell it
- Your desired profit margin. A reasonable margin is 50% plus.
- The Recommended Retail Price (RRP)

The following example will show how to use this information to determine your profit and therefore your profit margin.

i See chapter... ◎ Get it done ♀ Thinking time ■ Example ☺ You can do it!

■ **Example**

Information you need to have; example figures...

Supplier / Wholesale Price	£2.99
Postage & Packaging (P&P)	£5.00 for 10 items (50p each)
VAT charged on purchase	17.5%
Profit Margin	50%
Staff Commission	5%
RRP	£9.99

Cost of Item
The actual cost of the item to you is:-

Supplier / Wholesale item price	£2.99
P&P	£0.50
Total	£3.49
VAT	£0.61

Total you will pay for 1 item is £4.10
(Note: - the VAT is only a cost if you are not registered for VAT; please see *i* chapter 14 on Finance to understand how VAT works)

RRP (recommended retail price)
The RRP is the price the supplier suggests or insists you sell their product for. To calculate how much of that income goes to VAT you should divide the RRP or your selling price by 1.175.

In this example, the RRP or retail price is £9.99

£9.99 divided by 1.175 = £8.50 (this is how much belongs to your business after VAT; the £1.49 difference is the tax that goes to Customs & Excise)

Commission
In this example staff commission is set at 5%. This should be calculated

on the amount left after VAT has been removed.

So, to work out the commission you would multiply 8.50 by 5%
£8.50 x 5% = £0.43 to the staff member who made the sale.

So selling the item at its recommended retail price of £9.99 will make you the following profit:-

£8.50 (£9.99 minus VAT) - £0.43 (staff commission) - £4.10 (item cost) + £0.61 (VAT you paid when you bought it returned) = **£4.51 Profit**

In this example, the RRP has provided a healthy profit margin of around 53%, so it's a good price.

Profit Margin Calculation
(£4.51 profit ÷ £8.50 price) x 100 = 53%

If the recommended retail price doesn't give you a good profit margin of between 40% to 60% then get to a price that does and assess whether it is a good price for the product. Obviously if you overprice it, you won't sell very many!

Finally, make your products make money for you!

MONEY MAKER NUMBER 3 - RENTING OUT SALON SPACE, DURING TRADING HOURS

In return for an agreed commission you could offer your salon space to self-employed beauty professionals or to doctors who offer specialist skin aesthetics treatments. Treatments such as Botox®, semi-permanent makeup, fillers and laser skin treatments are popular and quite pricey, therefore just booking a few clients a week on behalf of the doctor or self-employed beauty professional could significantly increase your revenue at no extra cost to you.

Beware; make sure you choose good people to work from your premises! Don't forget that from a client's point of view this person is a member of your team and represents your brand; the client trusts you to only provide them with good quality. Check references, certificates, licenses and insurance.

MONEY MAKER NUMBER 4 - RENTING OUT SALON SPACE, OUT OF HOURS

You could consider the option of renting out the whole or part of your salon space when it's not in use. For instance there may be people who need a space to have meetings or other business people who need to train staff and don't have an appropriate location. You could charge by the hour or evening and earn your business extra revenue. I would recommend you take a deposit in case any items are damaged.

MONEY MAKER NUMBER 5 - SELLING ADVERTISING

This is an interesting option if you have a busy salon or a large client list. Installing a plasma screen or advertising board in your salon can be very lucrative. It doesn't have to be too *in-your-face* and can be inline with the general decor of your place. If or when you are well established and have a large client mailing list you can offer other non competing businesses the opportunity to have their logo and a few short sentences about them at the bottom of your client newsletter or on your web site.

MONEY MAKER NUMBER 6 - PARTNERSHIPS WITH LOCAL BUSINESSES

Try partnering with other local businesses that complement yours by offering free or discounted treatments with a purchase of one of their services or products and vice versa. So for instance if you are a nail salon and next door you have a hairdressers then you could have a partnership whereby every client that has a full set of nails gets a free blow dry next door and every client that has a full colour and cut gets a free express manicure. This is a great way to build relationships and gain new clients.

Also consider you local chemist, flower or gift/card shop and the types of exchanges you can negotiate with them.

MONEY MAKER NUMBER 7 - WEB SITE

Every business should have an online presence. Close to 30 million people use the internet in the UK today and this number is ever increasing. If you sell products in your salon, then you can sell them online. To encourage salon clients to make that purchase with you, even when they can't get to the shop, offer them free delivery with a special salon-regulars code. Advertise your web site address on your outdoor signage so that drivers and passers-by can find out more about you when they get home or to their office. It's easier to remember a web address than a telephone number!

i See chapter... ◎ Get it done ♀ Thinking time ■ Example ☺ You can do it!

At Miss Salon™ we design and build tailor-made web sites from £420

Chapter Summary

These money making ideas are not the only ones out there; you need to put your creative thinking hat on and devise all sorts of ways to generate revenue. Remember that making money is the name of the game and you need to be smart, savvy and open minded about all your options. Think through your revenue streams now, before you launch, and be in a better position to implement them efficiently and successfully.

Start thinking about the different ways in which your business can and will generate income!

Chapter 6
LOCATION, PREMISES
&
SHOP-FIT

My beautiful shop!

In this chapter I will talk about the importance of the location of your salon and discuss in detail the various aspects of choosing the right premises.

Consider the following:-

- Where is my salon going to be; Location of the premises?
- How much can I spend on rent, premiums (if any) and the deposit?
- What are the rates and other local authority charges?
- What are the buildings insurance costs?
- What work will need to be done to the premises; what condition is it in?
- Is the size of the shop suitable? You may require space for treatment area(s), retail display area, reception area, customer waiting area, WC and staff room
- Are there facilities in place; WC, showers, kitchen etc?

LOCATION OF THE PREMISES

Location is everything! Open the most beautiful salon, providing the best treatments, on a quite remote road that no one can find and you are doomed. That ones pretty obvious, but what about the not so obvious, like the road just off a busy high street or the top floor or back-end of a shopping centre? You may not be as doomed, but you will have to work twice as hard to get people to notice you.

Remember that in this section we are talking about location and not the actual premises. Before you start your search make a list of the things you are looking for in your ideal location. Does it need to be close to home? Do you already have a client base, if so then does the shop need to be located close to most of your clients? Do you need parking? Is it in the congestion charge zone? What about competition; do you want to be located close to a competitor? Is the shops postal code important to the clientele that you want to market to and therefore attract?

Once you have established the criteria for your ideal location, list them in order of importance then start making your enquiries.

Do your own research!

Research Tips And Questions To Get Answered

What is the foot-fall traffic like on a Monday afternoon, Saturday, Wednesday, etc? What are the busy times; peak and off-peak times?

Is there parking? How much does it cost per hour? Is there a cost associated with entering the zone/area? Congestion charge, entry fees, etc. How could these costs affect your customer's salon spending power or their thoughts on value for money? Are there good public transport links to the salon?

Is it a predominantly residential or commercial area? Are people working, living, visiting or travelling through there? What are property prices like in the area? This can help to indicate the salary brackets of the residents and their general status and spending priorities; young families, singles, students, mature residents, etc.

What about opening hours? Department stores, shopping centres and malls have specific opening hours that may or may not be good for your business.

Are there other salons on the same street, building or floor? Are they offering the same services and products you plan to offer? Does business look good for them? Are they busy? Being located near to a competitor is not necessarily a bad thing; just think of how many petrol stations, pizza restaurants or grocery shops you've seen in one area. In America I have seen six nail salons on one street! A variety of similar offerings brings more customers to the area; but don't choose be near too much competition.

Ask locals, the landlord and estate agents these questions but do your own research by visiting and observing the area over a period of time and answer these questions yourself.

THE LEASE, RENT, DEPOSIT AND PREMIUMS

The first questions to ask about any premises are how much does it cost (rent & rates, deposit and premiums) and for how long can I have it (the length of the lease)?

The Lease

Regarding the lease, the basics are:-

Professional help
An experienced commercial property solicitor and a surveyor are vital for a smooth exchange of contracts. Make sure they explain all aspect of the lease, highlighting anything unusual about it or the building and its structure before you sign it.

Duration
A lease can be any length of time. Think about the amount of money and marketing effort you will put into the property and weigh this up with the length of the lease. Also think about the potential risks of the business not being successful and weigh that up with being bound to the property through a long lease. Fortunately you can negotiate and add-in a 'break clause' which will allow you a notice period in which to 'break' the lease. So, for example, you could have a 5 year lease with a 2 year break clause. This means that you can use and are responsible for payment on the property for 5 years,

however if you need to, you can leave after 2 years if you give 6 months notice (usually) to the landlord at 18 months into the lease. Having a break-clause is important and can be very handy if things don't go as planned, so make sure you get one.

> **Remember**
> Everything is negotiable and you must get the best advice and understanding you can from an experienced commercial property solicitor. They can highlight where other landlords have been flexible in other deals and what responsibilities you are taking on.

Other major lease considerations will be your Health and Safety responsibilities, buildings insurance, maintenance responsibilities (internal/external repairs) and dilapidation.

You may be credit scored when going for a lease and some landlords want rent guarantees.

In most cases the landlord is represented by the estate agent. The landlord can be an individual, a small company or a large organisation. This can have a large effect on the speed and flexibility of your negotiations.

Sometimes you may be taking over a lease from another business and not directly from the landlord (but with the landlords consent). These exchanges could have premiums attached to them, as the shop is in great condition, or could be really beneficial to you, as the tenants are desperate to leave and throw in the deposit. All circumstances are different.

Just be smart and confident enough to find out how far you can get with your negotiations. Meet the lessees and find out their motives for leaving. Are there any other interested parties? Are the lessees in a hurry to leave? These factors can affect their flexibility.

The Rent

Most rent on commercial properties is paid three months in advance. Try and see if you can negotiate an initial rent free period with the landlord. Usually you can try and get the refurbishment/decoration period rent free, as it is clear that you will not be making any money during that time and the rent can be quite a burden during the shop-fit stage. I have heard of lease exchanges where the landlord has agreed to the first 6 months rent free! This can be the case if the property is particularly run down and requires a lot of work before it will be ready for business.

The Deposit

The deposit is usually three months rent. This is quite a large initial expense, so keep it in mind when looking for premises.

Premiums

A premium on a property is an amount of money that the landlord or current lessee puts on a lease exchange when a shop has certain tangible and in-tangible benefits.

■ Example

If you find a property that was recently a beauty salon and already has built in showers with pressure pumps, separate treatment rooms and a well established clientele, then it would be understandable that the tenants may want a cash lump sum to pay for those benefits.

Section Summary

Depending on your negotiating skills and power, the total initial cost of signing a lease will be the sum of the following:-

- Between 1 to 3 months rent
- Between 1 to 3 months rent as deposit
- Any premium
- Solicitor's fees
- Surveyor's fees

THE RATES AND OTHER LOCAL AUTHORITY CHARGES

Business Rates

Like Council Tax (UK) for domestic properties, businesses pay Business Rates, also called Non-Domestic Rates. These are a big consideration for any business. Business Rates are a local tax that businesses and other occupiers of non-domestic properties pay to the council as a contribution towards the costs of local authority services such as police and fire fighting. I was paying just over £2,500 a year in rates on my Fulham salon; this is a substantial addition to the rent.

Either the landlord or the tenants, of a commercial property, are responsible for paying the rates. Your rent may already include the rates and therefore the landlord will be responsible for paying the rates, otherwise you will have to ensure that you pay the business rates.

There is a lot more information on Business Rates, how they are calculated and how to pay them on the Business Link web site.

UK Readers
Visit www.businesslink.gov.uk and type in 'Business Rates' in the search bar.

---

 i See chapter... ◎ Get it done 💡 Thinking time ■ Example ☺ You can do it!

Other Council Charges

There are other council costs that you should investigate when assessing a property. Waste disposal, special treatments licensing and the costs associated with meeting your health and safety requirements (e.g., fire equipment, electrical equipment and maintenance, etc); see *i* chapter 15 on Health & Safety, Insurance and Licensing.

THE CONDITION IT'S IN

In this section I am referring to the walls, floors, ceiling, windows, etc; things that you cannot take away with you if you leave. The condition of the property is obviously an important consideration as it affects your start-up cost greatly! Do you have a budget for the internal and external decoration of the shop? Can the works that are required for this particular shop be done within the budget?

SIZE AND FACILITIES

The size of the shop you go for is subject to the kind of salon and types of treatments you want to give. Just keep in mind that you want to have enough room for the following salon areas:-

- The facilities – WC, showers, kitchen etc
- Treatment area(s)
- Retail display area
- Reception area
- Customer waiting area
- Staff room

Each of these spaces is addressed in later sections of the book. Have a rough idea of the measurements of your treatment tables, nail stations, hair stations, wash stations, reception desk, waiting area furniture, display shelves, etc, then with the shop floor-plans or dimensions, do a rough sketch of your shop fit.

◎ Get 3 recommended builders or shop fitters in to give you their quotes and duration for the work so that you have this information in mind during any planning and negotiations.

PLANNING YOUR LAYOUT, FURNITURE, FIXTURES AND FITTINGS

Using the space you have effectively; maximising on the profitability of every square metre, is very important. Getting this right first time will save you the very costly exercise of rectifying layout and furniture mistakes.

Personal experience

When I opened my first nail bar I didn't know that I needed to have in-built ventilators in the nail desk to meet the licensing criteria for the London borough I was in! This meant I had to have the entire nail bar table top re-made to include cut outs for the individual extractor fans. This cost me a whooping £3,000 within my first 6 weeks of opening!! Nightmare!

Six months after opening I realised that I also needed to have a retail display area because it became clear that treatments alone were not going to provide enough income. I hadn't planned this in my original layout and shop-fit, hence I was left needing to create makeshift displays on the actual nail bar table top which were obviously not as attractive as they needed to be! Another nightmare and wasted revenue opportunity.

Needless to say, all my subsequent nail bars were perfectly designed! No more costly design mistakes!

Planning Your Layout

Know what treatments you are going to offer, determine which ones you think are going to be the most profitable and cut up your floor space accordingly.

Try and fit in as many Money Making Stations (MMS) into the space you have, always keeping your salons financial goals and customer service objectives in mind.

As a guide use 60% of your floor space on salon services (including retail), 20% on your reception area (including retail) and the remaining 20% on washroom, client coats cupboard, staff room, office and salon storage (although storage solutions can also be cleverly added throughout the salon).

You could also use an architect to plan your salons layout. Note that some shop-fitting companies have in-house architects and offer planning and design as part of the package.

Sourcing and Choosing Your Fixtures and Fittings

Depending on your budget you can fit out your salon in two ways, either have furniture specially made for you or buy ready made pieces. Your marketing plan and budget will help you choose what you need and can afford for your business.

Remember when creating your perfect salon to think very carefully about:-

- Comfort
- Storage
- Cleaning
- Ease of use
- A typical clients journey through your salon from start to finish; coats, bags, payment, washing, etc

Your actual work stations, above all, need to be practical and fit for purpose. Just like you did when creating your first stock list, go through all the steps of a treatment and think about what furniture would make performing it comfortable for both the operator and the client. If you are an already experienced beauty professional then you will know what fixtures and fittings have made your job more enjoyable in the past. But even so, the little things can be missed, like the correct pedicure, hair or waxing trolley height, the correct drawer height for the tallest bottle in use, suitable bins for the different types of waste disposal, enough leg room, enough space to move around easily, countertop wells for hairdryers, etc. By thinking through and knowing the treatment process properly you can start to design your workstations for maximum benefit.

Work stations need to be:-

- Able to accommodate all that is required to perform a treatment
- Very well organised
- Easily put away
- Easily accessed
- Easy to clean
- Comfortable, not just for your clients but also for your staff
- Out of sight when not in use (optional)

Here Are A Few Tips On Sourcing Your Shop-Fit:-

- Look online; search for salon furniture, salon and spa designs, etc. You will get a selection of worldwide companies that have ready made furniture and equipment for you to purchase. Seeing the selection online can give you many ideas for how to fit-out your salon

- You could also consider having some of the furniture you see replicated with slight modification to suit your needs more. This could be done by a local carpenter or furniture maker; prices vary but worth investigating as an option.

- Search online for professional shop-fitters or shop design companies. These people specialise in creating your whole look and fitting your shop. Make sure you get quotes from at least 3 such companies. See more on this in *i* chapter 15, Hiring Professionals.

Keep in mind that there may be long waiting times for furniture. Be sure to order in time for your launch.

YOUR OFFICE

You may not have enough space in your salon to have your office, so it may need to be in your home. Either way you will need to have a working desk somewhere to do your paperwork.

As a minimum, your office will need the following:-

- A desk and chair
- A calendar
- A diary
- Pen holder
- A phone with fax, photocopier and answering service
- A computer with broadband connection
- A colour printer
- Desk lamp
- An in-tray
- An out-tray
- A bin
- Stationery, including envelopes, printer paper, writing paper, pens, pencils, stapler, ruler, erasers, cello tape, blue tack, metal clips, metal grips, folders, transparent folders and holders
- Notice board
- A lockable filing cabinet

THE SHOP FRONT

Your shop front is super-duper important! It is your welcome and your continuous advert!

Signage

Once you have decided on your business name and had a logo created use this logo on your shop front sign along with a very brief description in smaller letters. For example, a business called "Indulge Me" should have "Massage Makeup Hair Nails" in smaller letters under the name to help passers-by know what's on offer. On the other hand if your salon name is more descriptive, like Nail Haven, then this isn't necessary.

Your online web address and telephone number should also be displayed along with the name. Web addresses are much easier to remember than phone numbers, so be sure to have a web site with all the relevant info; see *i* chapter 13 and 16.

The Window, Entrance and Window Displays

I recommend that you keep your entrance and window free of too much information. I have driven past salons that have loads of different papers stuck on their windows - *with visible Blu-Tack no-less!! Come on now... if you can't make an effort with your displays clients may think you can't make an effort with them.* Other things carelessly plastered include opening and closing times, promotions, salon menu, beauty brands, images of models, job vacancies, CCTV threats(!) and more - *what a mess!* Too much info, badly presented can just turn potential clients off. Sometimes just being able to see inside the salon through a clean window is enough to gain a visit.

The entrance and the window displays are your on-going advert and

it is paramount that they are as clear and as attractive as possible. Design the layout of your shop front on paper first. Do a mock drawing of it including the sign (or where it will be), the door, window, etc, then place the following items:-

Area 1 - Information that rarely changes...
* A clear and well presented logo/salon name
* Include (if necessary) a short, sharp, enticing strap-line
* Your web address and phone number
* Your regular opening hours
* Open / Close sign

Area 2 - Information that changes often...
* A 3-item list of the treatments, services or products you offer that are new, unique or just plain popular
* A sub-headline that asks a question or highlights your salons' speciality.

Area's 1 and 2 should help you think of your shop front in the same way as a fashion store - Sign and standard info always the same and in the same place; fashion on mannequins always changing but in the same place. **In both of these be creative, be exciting and talk to the customers need.** Also, remember to have the windows and entrance cleaned often!

Chapter Summary

Just like committing to buying a house, choosing and leasing premises for your business will be one of the first, most costly and important decisions you will have to make. You really should have a good idea of the types of treatments, clientele and spending limit you are aiming for when you set out to hunt for premises. That way you will be less likely to make bad decisions or be bamboozled by estate agents. It is also very important to have an experienced solicitor and surveyor working for you in this transaction. See *i* chapter 16 on Hiring Professionals.

Chapter 7
STAFF

The heart of your business and your biggest on-going concern!

Hiring & Keeping Staff

Hiring and keeping the right staff for your business will undoubtedly be your biggest on-going challenge.

In terms of **hiring**, you will need to be thorough in your employment process; clear on what your business requires and can afford, and ensure your staff understand and are happy with all aspects of their employment. In terms of **keeping** staff, you will need to adopt a fair, consistent as well as flexible management style that your team can thrive under. **We will look at both aspects separately.**

HIRING STAFF

In this section we will look at how to employ good beauty professionals!

The Starter Pack

For the sake of sanity and one less thing to worry about after you launch, I highly recommend producing a Starter Pack for all new employees.

Each Starter Pack should contain the following:-

- An interview form
- A contract of employment (not completed)
- A copy of your Staff Handbook or Employment Guide (You can purchase a sample Miss Salon Staff Handbook for £9.99 from www.misssalonbusiness.com)
- Health and Safety Induction sheet
- Payroll forms
- A check list

The starter pack will help you keep track of the different stages of the employment process and make sure that all the necessary forms are completed and the right actions taken. After the person has joined the company, their starter pack can become part of their record file.

Minimum Employment Criteria

I recommend that you set your company criteria for recruiting salon staff; this will help you or any one in charge of hiring keep focused on what you are really looking for in a candidate, especially during the interview.

◎ Outline on one page what the **Essential Criteria** and **Desirable Criteria** are that salon employees should have.

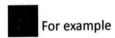 For example

Essential Criteria may be...

* Have all the correct qualifications
* Have previous hands-on salon experience
* Have a genuine interest in people
* Have adequate verbal communication skills
* Have a smart appearance with a polite and helpful manner
* Be flexible to working within trading hours of the salon
* Have plenty of stamina

Desirable Criteria may be...

* Retail sales experience
* Have training in sales and service skills or a suitable retail qualification (see below)

- Have an interest in the products they sell
- Have experience in working with a team
- Have experience in working to targets
- Have experience with handling stock, deliveries, processing orders
- Be competent at using computerised equipment such as cash tills and good mental arithmetic skills.

Referring to this criteria during the recruitment process can save you time and keep you focused; ultimately helping you hire the best possible staff for your business.

Deciding On Staffing Levels

How many people do you need? I would create a few test rotas. Depending on your opening hours, days and work stations, you should try and fill the spaces with all full-timers, then do a few different combos of a mixture of full-time and part-time staff. By doing this, you will find your ideal scenario, giving you an idea of how many people you will need to recruit.

■ If your salon is open 7 days a week from 9am to 8pm you are going to struggle to staff it with just full-time staff, they will either work too many hours and burnout or you won't be able to fulfill their weekly hour requirements. These sort of trading hours will require a mixture of full and part time staff. Also see *i* chapter 10, On-going Management.

Advertising For Staff

Place ads in beauty industry magazines, web sites and in local newspapers.

A great, very reasonably priced web site for finding beauty professionals in the UK is www.hairandbeautyjobs.com

Super Tip...
Advertise for salon staff for free! Get online and seek out forums and networks for beauty professionals. For example www.salongeek. com and www.nailgeek.com are very popular communities of beauty pros who may be interested in your job offer.

A simple recruitment ad should include your company logo, description of the jobs available, some information on your minimum requirements, job location, a contact name and number.

Using A Recruitment Agency To Find Staff

There are recruitment agencies that can put forward a few candidates for potential employment. They usually charge a fee to register with them and then a further fee or salary percentage when/if you chose to employ the candidate. This can be quite high and a really wasted cost if that candidate leaves your company shortly after joining.

I have found that agencies are great for filling short term staffing gaps like, holidays, unexpected absences, etc.

The Interview Process

The interview process should be split into 4 parts.

Part 1 – Initial telephone conversation
• Ask about qualifications and experience (the essential criteria questions that don't require face to face)

• Explain the interview process; for instance if you plan to do a

trade-test, the fact that the interview will not continue if the trade-test is unsuccessful, if they need to bring any of their own tools, bring their CV (Resume), certificates and photos, how long they can expect to be interviewed for, etc

- Arrange a date, time and location for the interview

- Answer any questions they may have about the job, salary, company, etc

Part 2 – The trade-test
See below.

Part 3 – The interview
When the candidate arrives for their interview ensure that you take the time to make them feel comfortable. Introduce yourself and make light conversation about their journey and the weather. Talk through the interview process again. See more on the interview below.

Part 4 – Hiring and first day
See below.

The Trade-Test
My biggest time saving tip is to do a 'trade-test' straight away! There is absolutely no point in going through the interview questions, chatting about this and that, only to discover the manicurist can't paint to save her life! Save time by starting the interview with a 'trade-test'.

A trade-test is simply an opportunity for the applicant to show you their practical treatment skills. So if you are looking for a nail technician, ask her to paint your nails. If you are looking for a beauty therapist, ask her to give you a face massage, wax your arm and so on. Assess how competent and experienced they are by their performance. Anyone who is good at what they do will be able to demonstrate their expertise in just a few minutes. Expect high standards and professional behaviour during this test. Mark their performance out of 10.

The Interview
Once you have established that the applicant has potential...

...applies the right amount of pressure in a massage, waxed a body part thoroughly, shaped your eyebrows well, painted a French polish perfectly, showed excellent control when handling your hands and fingers while applying the polish, spoke confidently and clearly about what she/he was doing to you...

...and you would be happy to either invest time in training her on your planned treatment methods or be happy for her to work on a paying customer, then go ahead with the full interview.

Using your pre-prepared Starter Pack, now assigned to this particular candidate, complete the interview form while you talk to them.

Interview questions should include the following:-

- Personal details (name, address, telephone, national insurance number, date of birth and bank details)

- What industry qualifications do they have? Ask to see all her certificates and take photocopies. Make sure that her qualifications comply with any licensing requirements that your local council may request. See *i* chapter 15 on Government Regulations.

- How many years experience and the relevance and quality of the experience? You want to hire people with at least 2 years relevant salon experience. Someone who qualified as a beauty therapist 2 years ago but has spent her time doing facials for friends and family only is not going to have the same high quality experience as someone who gained the same qualifications, started as a salon apprentice and slowly worked her way up to treating paying customers in a supportive environment. However, some people can be very gifted and perform very well even with little

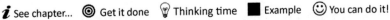

experience; make an assessment keeping their trade-test results in mind.

- More details; ask a series of questions that help you establish more about the character, personality, ambitions and motivations of the candidate.

  ◼ For example
  - Why did you become a beauty therapist, hairdresser, nail technician, etc?
  - Do you enjoy your job?
  - What is the best thing about your job?
  - What are you really good at?
  - What is good customer service? Have you ever been in a difficult situation with a customer? How did you handle it?
  - What do you want to be doing in 5 years time?
  - What skills would you like to learn?
  - Why are you leaving your current job?
  - Why do you want to work in this salon?
  - How much stamina is required in your current job? Is it a busy salon? Do you have to multi-task?
  - Do you enjoy retailing products?
  - Why do you think it is important as a professional beauty therapist, hairdresser, nail technician, etc to retail products?

  ...and so on

- Other basics
  - What hours?
  - What days?
  - Is there flexibility in the above?
  - What was/is previous/current pay rate?
  - What is the notice period for their current job? When can they start?

- Can they provide references?

Some Key Points To Remember

- The interviewee should do most of the talking – remember to ask open questions in order to investigate as much information as you can about their skills and experience.

- Listen carefully to the answers and make notes.

- Ensure you ask questions to fill in any blanks that may appear in their CV/application form.

- Make sure that you ask all the relevant questions regarding the hours of work, flexibility, etc

- Ensure that the questions you have planned to ask will gain the information you need to establish if the candidate meets your set criteria.

Hiring And Their First Day

When you decide to hire the applicant give them a salon price list plus any other salon literature and their copy of the Staff Handbook and Contract from their Starter Pack to read before their start date.

Arrange a start date.

Their first day / week at work should be an introduction to your salon, your methods and practices and a time to conclude all the new starter paperwork, including signing the contract, completing payroll forms from your accountant or payroll provider like Ceridian in the UK (www.ceridian.co.uk) and completing the salon Health & Safety induction. If you have a training programme (see below) this would be the time to go through it.

 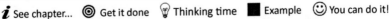

"A smooth and organised start is the best way to introduce a new person to your business. Start as you mean to go on!"

Hiring Staff vs Renting Out Salon Space To Self-Employed Beauty Professionals

What's better? This depends entirely on your own business needs and model. Here are some pros and cons of renting out space:-

Renting pros...

- No staff salaries (big pro!)
- Regular and constant income from space
- No employment contracts
- No employers national insurance contributions
- No payroll
- The rental rate can include the cost of products and equipment used

Renting cons...

- Reduced sense of team spirit, leading to an everyman for himself salon culture (big con!)
- Reduced control on staff start times, affecting the 'walk-in' service and general customer service
- Renting out space means financial growth limited; rental income stays the same even if salon gets busier. Having said that, this can be addressed by making the rent a percentage of turnover rather than a fixed amount. So when the salon gets busier and business gets better for the individual, you benefit from this also. This deal though, may seem unfair, if the individual's sales

increase due solely to their hard work and abilities and not due to any extra marketing efforts on your part.

- Reduced control on standards and products used, however this can also be addressed by agreeing to a set treatment procedure.

If you choose the space rental route, then be sure to work out the right amount to charge for the space. Start with a figure that is correct for your business, changing or increasing this later will be difficult without potentially spoiling relationships. See *i* chapter 14, Finance and Accounting.

Hiring The Wrong Person!

People with a poor sense of duty and work ethic will only bring you, your team and your business down. Unfortunately this does happen and I just can't stress enough how awful this can be. Staff who are constantly off sick, don't do their tasks on the rota, constantly late to work, have a bad attitude towards customers and so on are just a liability and it's really important that you manage this in the correct way and fast!

Protect yourself and your business by setting up a trial period, clearly stated in the handbook that all new employees are subject to. If you are unhappy then you should be able to let them go, within that period, without notice and without having to go through the disciplinary procedure. At the moment that period is within the first 1 month of employment. However check and double check this with current employment law.

Having said that, when you become an experienced employer, you will be able to tell within the first couple of weeks whether or not someone is right for your business; if you smell a rat, I strongly advice you to let them go early, early, early! Don't hang on thinking that they'll get better; they won't. If they are poor at the start of a job they will only get worse, especially the more irritated you get! If,

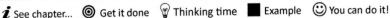

however, they are well into their employment then you will have to refer to your disciplinary procedure.

For UK readers, visit...

Advisory, Conciliation and Arbitration Service - ACAS
ACAS aims to improve organisations and working life through better employment relations.
www.acas.org.uk

Department of Business Enterprise and Regulatory Reform - BERR
www.berr.gov.uk

KEEPING STAFF

So now that you have spent time hiring the perfect person, how do you ensure you keep them motivated and happy to work hard for the business? Remember that a constant turnover of staff is very costly to any business and can lose you customers.

Most business owners from all industries will tell you that their biggest problems are staff related. Well of course it would be staff related, after all, these are human beings we are talking about; full of complexities, mood swings and changing needs!

It takes patience, great interpersonal skills and advanced management techniques to consistently be able to motivate, drive and develop your team of staff. The difficulty is that you are only human too with your own stresses and mood swings! However if you are taking on the job of manager / business owner, you are taking on a difficult role which will require you to rise above all of your own personal issues and always be objective, consistent, patient and competent at looking after your team and your business.

A Few Staff Management Tips

Staff management is the area I believe is most ignored by entrepreneurs when driven by the great excitement of starting your own business. You think that everyone will share your enthusiasm for the shop and work as hard as you to make it a success. Why not, it's the best shop in the world and your blood, sweat and tears have built it and everyone else is going to see that... right? No, not right!

Most people that come to you for a job are doing just that, looking for a job; not a business to run, not a highly-driven, excited boss to deal with!

Firstly, they want to know their exact job description, hours of work, how much they are going to get paid, when and how they will get paid and any other information that could ultimately affect their 'rice-bowl', i.e., their income!

Secondly, they may be career minded and want to know if there are any opportunities for promotion in your business.

The subject of employee/people management is a huge one which people study and train for years to perfect. I can't teach you how to manage staff in one chapter however I will highlight some invaluable skills, tools and techniques that make good managers and get the best out of your team.

- Have a Staff Handbook – leave confusion at the door!

- Have formal individual performance reviews

- Set targets, both salon and individual; give your team a goal

- Introduce incentives to achieve targets

- Have regular staff meetings

 See chapter... Get it done 💡 Thinking time ■ Example ☺ You can do it!

- Always praise and show appreciation for a job well done

- Only reprimand staff in private and never ever on the shop floor

- Exercise patience and show understanding

- Actively listen to problems, concerns and criticism – Seek to understand and then to be understood

- Keep your word and always be trustworthy and reliable

- Practise what you preach and always set a good example

- Don't take criticisms from staff personally; they are airing their views about the behaviour of their manager / boss, not about you as an individual

- Treat every team member as you would like to be treated

- Be hands-on with salon jobs

- Don't shout, use bad language or be sarcastic when speaking to your team

- Don't disappear from the salon for hours on end saying you have loads of paperwork; this is never appreciated especially if business is not so good and your team need you there to keep them motivated and show them what to do to improve things. You can do you paperwork after hours.

- Remember that you are the leader and how you treat your staff and behave in front of them is how they will conduct themselves in front of your customers!

Also see *i* chapter 1, You – The Business Owner

Recommended Reading On Management And Leadership

There are many great books on how to be a good manager and leader. Some of the best ones I have found are:-

- One Minute Manager by Kenneth Blanchard
- Leadership and The One Minute Manager by Kenneth Blanchard
- Principle-Centred Leadership by Stephen Covey

These books and many others are available to purchase from the **Miss Salon™ Blog** on www.misssalon.blogspot.com. Visit the blog to read more tips, get advice and ask questions.

OTHER STAFF RELATED TOPICS

Staff Handbook

A staff handbook is an employee's guide to your company policies and practices; it clearly defines their job roles and it usually forms part of their employment contract.

You can buy an example of a full staff handbook plus employment contract from www.misssalonbusiness.com for £9.99

When creating your staff handbook, consider some of the following headings:-

- Welcome note
- Salon practises
- Therapist's duties and job descriptions

 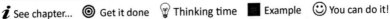

- Salon co-ordinator (receptionists) duties and job description
- Normal salon opening hours
- Shifts
- Rota
- Lateness
- Overtime
- Lunch and breaks
- Absence due to illness / Sick Leave
- Unauthorised absence
- Uniforms / dress code
- Health and safety procedure
- Customer care and complaints
- Appointment system / taking customer details
- Use of company facilities and products
- Probation period
- Leaving the company
- Grievance procedure
- Disciplinary procedure
- Termination of contract; notice periods
- Salary details; pay dates and method
- Commission rate
- Bonus scheme – 10% team bonus
- Holiday leave
- Maternity leave
- Responsibilities to the company
- Managers
- Contacts

Wages and Payroll

Investigate the rate of pay for therapists in your salons area. Offer a competitive wage; maybe including commission and other incentives. Do not overpay unless they are literally going to bring celebrities to your salon every week! Do not get sucked into trying to excite a potential employee into accepting a position in your salon and over promise on pay or future rises or promotions. When deciding on what financial incentives/rewards to offer, start by looking at your business costs and work out what you can afford to pay per target level. See *i* chapter 14, Financials and Accounting

The payroll should be handled by a payroll company or your accountant. They will advise you on all the information you will need to get from your new employee and provide you with forms that you can have ready to complete in the Starter Packs.

Pay can be weekly, bi-weekly or monthly. You can decide what's best for you. Just remember that if you are paying commission and your payroll company have been instructed to calculate and pay wages via bank transfer, you will need to have totalled the commission at least 4-5 days in advance of pay day. This means that if you are paying bi-weekly, then your staff will be paid 2 weeks wages for work they did 4-5 days ago. For ease I would set it a week back.

■ **Example**
Say staff salaries are paid every two weeks on a Friday and today is pay day, Friday 27 July.

Sally worked on the 11, 12, 13, 18, 19, 20, 25, 26 and 27th July.

The current 2 week pay run is from Friday 6 July to Thursday 19 July; as outlined on the calendar on the next page.

It takes 1 week to collect all the staff hours, calculate all the commission, send totals to a payroll company, produce payslips and transfer funds to staff accounts in time for the Friday's payday.

On the 27th, Sally can expect to be paid for the work she did in that 2 week pay period, i.e. 11, 12, 13, 18 and 19. The next 2 week pay period runs from the 20th July to 2nd August. She will then get paid for the work she did on the 20, 25, 26 and 27... and so on.

Once you have established how often you want to pay your staff and for what period you should create 'pay sheets' to help you

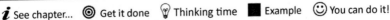

JULY						
Sun	Mon	Tues	Wed	Thurs	Fri	Sat
1	2	3	4	5	Start 6	7
8	9	10	11 Sally	12 Sally	13 Sally	14
15	16	17	18 Sally	End 19 Sally	20 Sally	21
22	23	24	25 Sally	26 Sally	27 Sally	28
29	30	31				

calculate their total hours, days off, sick days, commission, etc for that period.

Pay sheets can be created from a combination of the rota and sales logs; please see *i* chapter 11, On-going Management for how this is done. Once created the relevant information should be sent to a payroll company or accountant for processing.

Performance Reviews

A performance review is a formal way of assessing how an individual is doing against an agreed set of criteria.

It is important to set up formal staff performance reviews for the following reasons:-

- It helps the employee to better understand the expectation of their role

- It provides the employee and employer with the opportunity to

see how they have developed over time

- It identifies specific areas for improvement; both for the employee and employer

- It identifies areas of excellence and provides an opportunity for formal praise and reward

If you plan on giving pay rises or any other type of financial rewards, the best time for this may be after a good review, as there is a clear relationship between excellent performance and reward.

I recommend a performance review is scheduled every 6 months.

How are they conducted?
Before the review meeting:-
Talk through the review process, explaining how it works and what it aims to do. The staff member should be given the review questionnaire to complete at least a week in advance. The questionnaire should be completed by the individual and handed over to you for your comments on their performance.

At the review meeting:-
To get the best out of the session, try having this meeting in a relaxed environment; off the shop floor, maybe in a local coffee shop taking care not to be overheard.

During the review meeting, walk through the answers, discussing the various topics openly. Encourage the individual to share their views, ensuring that you actively listen before giving your opinion and suggested plan of action.

The review should be treated as confidential.

Conclude the meeting by summarising and confirming any next steps that may have come out of the discussion. Below are some questions that you may want to put in the performance review questionnaire:-

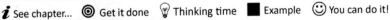 *i* See chapter...   Get it done Thinking time   Example   You can do it!

- Past experience - Please indicate your level of expertise and skill before you were employed by X, in all areas that you feel are relevant to your job.

- Current situation - What skills, if any, do you think you have gained since working at X?

- Please give yourself marks out of 10 for your performance on the following treatments and the average length of time they take you to do.

- Relationships - How is your relationship with your Manager? Please be more specific than 'good' or 'bad'. Indicate exactly what makes it a good or bad relationship. Also, how do you get on with your other colleagues?

- Working Environment - What is your overall impression of the salon? Please use adjectives to answer this question, for example, friendly, disorganized, intense, pleasant, efficient, trustworthy, untrustworthy, etc. Use as many words as you like. What do you think of the range of treatments? What do you think of the range of products; sold and used?

- Future – What are your future plans? Is X fulfilling your requirements? If not, then what is missing? Suggest improvements.

- Please give yourself marks out of 10 for the following skills:-
  - Team work
  - Customer service
  - Time keeping
  - Salon assistant
  - Product knowledge
  - Reliability
  - Personal organisation
  - Personal hygiene
  - Work area maintenance
  - Attention to detail

- Product adviser
- Treatment adviser

A complete Performance Review Questionnaire, which you can use in your salon, can be purchased from www.misssalonbusiness.com for £3.99

Staff Meetings

You should have staff meetings at least (at the very least) once a month.

Try to not spend the whole time talking about your business agenda and open the floor for all of the team to discuss any salon topics of importance to them. Listen to any suggestions and concerns objectively and always follow through with any actions you have promised to take.

Training

Training is another very important aspect of staff management. Even your finest therapists could do with refresher courses or extra customer service tips from time to time. Regularly carrying out staff performance reviews will highlight areas that need addressing.

Your team and new starters may require training initially and from time to time in the following 5 main areas:-

- Treatments
- Product retail
- Customer service
- Salon operations (till training, health & safety, station maintenance, etc)
- Teamwork

Depending on the number of staff in your salon, you may want to consider hiring a trainer to train staff in general and run your training programme, including reporting on staff progress throughout and undertaking the recruitment trade-tests.

Creating a training programme
To create a training programme for your business, write down all the tasks and responsibilities that each type of staff member may be assigned. Sort this list under the five areas mentioned earlier. Then plan how to execute training or showing new or existing staff how to go about doing a great job for your salon.

Make training sessions fun and effective. Check that the trainee is actually learning and understands what they are being taught. Role play can be a very effective training method.

Assuming that your hiring process and/or staff performance reviews are robust, you should already have a fair idea of the skill level of a particular staff member and therefore the areas that need training attention. I would suggest that all staff regardless of their skill level should go through some form of training in all of the 5 areas before they start their job. Better to have everyone singing from the same hymn sheet than not.

Your training programme should aim to achieve the following:-

• All treatments on your pricelist are performed in the same way each time by each therapist;

• Ensure that all your staff know and can effectively use tried and tested methods to sell products;

• Keep customer service standards high throughout your business; this is paramount!

• Create a team that know how the salon functions and are empowered to deal with any issues smoothly and properly.

- Create a team that look out for one another, are positive about the business, and so can be competitive without being negative.

Costs of training

You may choose to charge staff for certain parts of their training, for instance, you may stock a certain brand of skin care and need a staff member to have official training from the supplier; this may or may not incur expense, but if it does, it needs to be covered by the trainee as it is a transferable skill and qualification.

If you have a good new-starter training programme in place, you may want to stipulate in the contract that if a new-starter leaves the business within the first 6 months, they will be charged a set fee to cover costs for part of this salon training.

Who will pay for the training must be agreed or highlighted during the hiring process or pre-training.

Dress Codes and Uniform

A dress code and/or uniform is advisable. Formalising this will prevent any issues on the shop floor.

A dress code can address hair, jewellery, nails, shoes and clothes.

For instance, a hairdressing salon may have a dress code that says wear fashionable/trendy clothes and ensure your hair is well styled at all times when at work. Or a nail salon may require that the technicians keep short clean nails and have fresh breath... ! This is up to you and should be in keeping with the style of your business.

Targets

Salons should have both sales and customer service targets. Setting

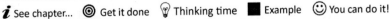

these targets gives everyone involved in the business something to aim towards; a clear goal post. Floating from one day to the next without any understanding of how the business is doing or how each staff member is performing can just get boring and meaningless. Please see *i* chapter 11, On-going Management on how to do this.

Sick Leave

I strongly recommend that you set-up a sickness policy. Sound, fair and consistent policies and procedures can provide a framework within which absence problems can be better handled.

Constant absenteeism is costly and can cause you a lot of stress. Your policy should include sick pay, when you require a doctor's certificate (usually after 7 consecutive days of illness) and how many days off sick within a set period will be tolerated before the disciplinary procedure is started. Also, be sure to keep very clear records of any absences from work. Importantly, see that your policy is fair to those who are genuinely sick.

More up-to-date information on this matter and employment law can be found on the Business Link and ACAS web sites.

Grievance, Disciplinary and Dismissal Procedure

Grievance Procedure

You should provide your team with a way to air their concerns in a confidential, structured and fair manner.

All employers must provide their employees with a written grievance procedure complying with the statutory standard grievance procedure [Reference www.businesslink.gov.uk]. This is best included in your staff handbook.

Disciplinary and Dismissal Procedure
A disciplinary and dismissal procedure should to be in place to handle matters of gross misconduct or poor performance.

All employers are required by law to set out their dismissal, disciplinary and grievance rules in writing for their employees. Failure to do this or to follow these procedures when dismissing an employee will result in extra compensation for the employee and the dismissal being held as automatically unfair *[Reference www. businesslink.gov.uk]*. This is best included in your staff handbook.

The best place for up-to-date information on this and how to go about creating your Grievance, Disciplinary and Dismissal Procedure visit:-

www.businesslink.gov.uk and select 'Employing People'
www.acas.org.uk, especially see 'Employment Forms'
www.direct.gov.uk and select 'Employment'

Employment Law and Keeping Up-To-Date

Employment law changes all the time and as an employer it is your duty to stay on top of these changes. Luckily, once you are a registered employer and making employer's national insurance contributions through the PAYE system, you will receive regular employment law update packs. You might also have a good employment law solicitor look at or maintain your staff contracts and handbook.

Being an employer is quite a responsibility and can be tough but there is plenty of information out there to support your new role.

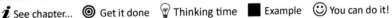 *i* See chapter... Get it done 💡 Thinking time ■ Example You can do it!

Chapter 8
STOCK

How to source, order and manage your stock

The salon's inventory!

This chapter will help you understand how to source, order and manage your stock.

CHOOSING PRODUCTS, BRANDS AND SUPPLIERS

The best place to start is at the beauty trade shows! All the top professional beauty brands and their distributors set-up stands at national trade shows, allowing salon owners and other beauty professionals the chance to browse their range, speak to brand representatives and buy.

Meeting your potential salon suppliers face to face is a great opportunity to introduce yourself and begin to establish what should be a long and prosperous business relationship; tell them your plans and see what they can do for you!

For your first visit go open-minded and collect all the information you can; take every leaflet, brochure, info pack and watch as many free demos as you can. Take the info home and study the leaflets, products and prices. For more, go online and see their web sites and search for even more suppliers. Compare quality and prices.

Make a list of your top ten.

On your next visit to the show, home-in on the products and suppliers of interest and ask all the questions you need answered.

■ For example
- Can they negotiate on price? Discounts on bulk orders maybe?
- What are their payment terms?
- What are their account opening procedures and requirements?
- What is their order process and how quickly can they deliver?
- What are their delivery charges?

i See chapter... ◎ Get it done 💡 Thinking time ■ Example ☺ You can do it!

- Do they need a minimum order?
- Will they provide free product training for your team?

Remember that for suppliers you are their business, you are their target market, you are their customer! If they are any good and worth working with, they will give you the time, attention and customer service you need, no matter how big or small your organisation is or will be.

A few trade show tips...

- Plan your day using the show guides
- Have plenty of rest the night before, arrive early and don't carry heavy handbags and other bits.
- Have a pen and paper
- Use the first day of the show as an opportunity to meet & greet and window shop; don't buy anything; save your money!
- Collect all the literature suppliers are giving out
- Go to the talks and seminars

Any national (and international) professional beauty shows can be found online and definitely at www.professionalbeauty.co.uk

Often, trade shows are very busy so if there isn't time on the day to discuss your potential relationship, then arrange to meet another time. Whatever you do, take your time in choosing the right products for your business. Ultimately you are planning to make a profit by using them, convincing your team to use them and selling them!

When choosing what brands to stock, keep in mind the following:-

- Is the product actually any good? Do the products have testimonials? Do they work and give excellent results?

- Are the products well packaged, i.e. easy to use? Can you get training?

- What is their brand power? Will the brand itself bring in business?

- What are the purchase costs and therefore treatment costs and retail costs? Can you, your customer, your location afford the brand?

See *i* chapter 5, Making Money - How will the cost of stock affect my treatment price list?

Extra money saving tip...

Don't buy your consumable items from a top brand distributor as they will most likely be the most expensive! Instead find a smaller beauty supplier for your cotton, paper roll and so on. If you can handle a variety of suppliers it would be prudent of you to source all your salons products at the lowest possible price. But remember that each supplier charges delivery fees and some offer discounts on larger orders so this should be taken into account when doing your costings.

PREPARING YOUR FIRST STOCK LIST AND ORDERING

By this stage you should have chosen your brands and suppliers and therefore have product samples, or even better, product training and have full supplier price lists with quantities in litres, ml and/or oz.

When preparing your first stock list start with your treatment list; go through each treatment step by step and make a note of all the products you will need to perform it, remembering every detail (like the funnel you will need to transfer liquids from your gallon/5 litre containers into your station size bottles).

i See chapter...　◎ Get it done　♀ Thinking time　■ Example　☺ You can do it!

Once you have completed this list, decide on the quantities of each item for your first order. Don't overstock your salon and therefore overspend. Aim to keep your capital and operational expenditure (see *i* chapter 14, Finances and Accounting) down and remember you can always buy more supplies later if you start to run out.

■ For example, your stock list/order sheet could look like this:-

Supplier	Quantity	Item	Price	Price +Tax	Total
Derma 0845 777 7777; Account No. 1234; Contact:- Jenny					
Derma	20	Clay Cleanser 100ml	£20.00	£23.50	£470.00
Derma	20	Active Moist 100ml	£20.00	£23.50	£470.00
Total	40				£940.00
Creative 0845 888 8888; Account No. 5678 Contact:- Susie					
Creative	10	Nail Fresh 50ml	£9.00	£10.75	£107.50
Creative	100	Nail Enamels 15ml	£2.50	£2.99	£299.00
...and so on					
Total	110				£406.50
TOTAL ORDER					£1,346.50

Retail Stock

Remember to also consider retail stock in your first list. It is best to purchase retail stock having planned how much display space you have and how you plan to merchandise. Again, don't order too much to start.

Ordering Stock

Ordering stock can actually be a lengthy exercise, especially if you have a long list of suppliers. Be systematic when ordering. As shown in the example stock list, have the supplier's name, telephone number and your account number all together. If you can, add a column with their product order codes as well; this usually helps speed up the order. As you order each item, confirm the price and tick it off. Make any changes and add any comments as you go along, for instance, items out of stock or incorrect pricing. Print off the full list when all your orders are complete.

Try and keep ordering stock down to once a month or every two weeks at the most after a full salon stock count.

Please note!

Suppliers show their prices excluding VAT (goods tax) and P&P (postage and packaging). Once you have totalled your order plus the P&P charge, add a further 17.5% tax onto that total for a true understanding of your final bill. If you are VAT registered you can claim this amount back from the taxman. See *i* chapter 14 for more on how VAT works.

Taking Delivery Of Your Order

You must check the actual delivery against your order sheet/stock list.

If you have a large salon or offer a wide range of treatments or have more than one salon, then monitoring orders and taking delivery of stock can be a detailed and lengthy process. Frequently orders arrive incorrect or are missing items and these need to be chased up, which can be a job in itself!

Whoever is in charge of stock ordering should also have a clear order follow-up process to chase late, incorrect, damaged or incomplete deliveries.

PAYING FOR STOCK

In theory, getting 14, 30 or 60 day payment terms with your suppliers benefits your cash flow; allowing time for the purchases to make money for you before needing to pay for them. However in practise this adds a ton of admin for you to take care of. Firstly you have to be meticulous with keeping track of all unpaid invoices and then when they become due sending out cheques or telephoning suppliers again. Also, the added stress of constantly having money outstanding can be immense. I recommend that you apply for a business credit card with a limit that reflects the amount you normally spend on your monthly stock bill. Use this card to pay for salon supplies only and pay it off in one lump sum monthly. This way you will still benefit from the 30 day relief on your cash flow but only have to make one payment. If however you can't get a business credit card then it's no bad thing to pay for all your stock straight away and have the peace of mind that you are not running up debt for your business.

See *i* chapter 14, Finance and Accounting for more on cash flow.

Larger organisations can afford accounts departments that can spend all day managing invoices. You are better off using your energy managing your staff and marketing your business effectively than worrying about the pile of invoices that need paying!

Top tip...

See if you can get **Sale or Return** arrangements for certain retail items. That way when you want to test the selling power of a new item you don't have to fear the financial commitment; if they sell then great, you have already paid for them. If they don't sell then give them back and get a refund.

Keeping Invoices and Receipts

When you make stock orders or pay for anything in your business you must keep all your invoices and receipts. Make sure that your suppliers send you invoices. I suggest that you get into the habit of stapling all the invoices to the relevant order sheet, ready for your accountant.

STOCK MANAGEMENT

Set Product Usage Standards

Effective stock management is very important for your businesses cash flow and profit margins. It is obvious to see that money is lost when stock is broken or stolen but it's not so obvious when it is being used excessively or incorrectly. I strongly recommend as the business owner that you know how to perform all the treatments you offer in your salon so as to determine and set a standard for product usage.

Remember when setting these guide lines to pay particular attention to the salon consumables such as couch roll, cotton, gauze pads, cotton buds, paper roll, acetone, disinfectants, etc. These can be some of the most misused and therefore costly items.

Personal experience

I remember having to constantly go over how Retention+ (the liquid) was used in the salon when doing a full set of acrylic nails. Some nail technicians would dip their entire brush into the liquid just to make a bead and then, after applying it to the nail, would wipe their brush clean and dry on the paper towel! At that rate, one full set of nails would require two full dampen dishes of liquid! I knew, and could demonstrate, that a full set rarely needed more than half a dampen dish of liquid. Paying attention to this level of detail helped to save

i See chapter...   ◎ Get it done   ♀ Thinking time   ■ Example   ☺ You can do it!

my salon money, as Retention+ is not a cheap salon item! Besides, it is bad practise to misuse liquid and all your staff should be open to learning better ways of performing treatments.

Stock Counts

Count your stock regularly; I would suggest on a weekly basis. Regular stock counting highlights any misuse, loss and replenishment requirements.

Keeping Good Records

Be organised with you stock records. Ensure you keep records of the following:-

- Stock counts by date of count
- Orders made
- Orders received
- Late, incorrect or incomplete deliveries
- Invoices paid
- Lost, broken, stolen or damaged stock (Accidents, waste and theft records)

Stock Discrepancies

Investigate if things don't seem right after a stock count. Depending on your findings, address any issues in the appropriate arena; privately, at a staff meeting or during training.

Chapter Summary

- Choose your suppliers and products carefully;
- Don't over stock and over spend; you can always order more later;
- Prepare your first stock list using your treatment list and with a budget in mind;
- Set usage standards; make sure staff know how you expect products to be used;
- Keep good records and be in control of your salons stock!

 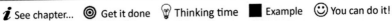

Chapter 9
RETAIL

Sell, Sell, Sell!

The only way to make any real money...

This may sound drastic but it's true. Better you understand this now and incorporate it into your plan, than realise it years later when you're wondering why you're not cash rich!

In general very few salon owners think of retail as a vital revenue stream for their business; with treatments usually providing over 90% of the salons income. I understand that you want to open a salon or a nail bar and not a shop, but I am here to tell you that sales from treatments alone are just not going to be enough in the long run. The difficulty though is that not many salon staff see themselves as sales people. However, **to be successful, you are going to have to take product sales seriously and work very hard at training your team to be sales people.**

Now when I say 'take product sales seriously' I don't mean you need to turn yourself and your team into wild animals and mall down every customer to buy buy buy! That just doesn't work. What I mean is that you will need to do three things:-

1. First, dedicate at least 30% of your salon space to retail; stands, displays, info, etc. In fact I would even go as far as to say, open a beauty-products shop and add a salon to it!! Basically, design the layout of your salon to attract customers, even if they don't want a treatment, just to browse through the products and ultimately, make a purchase.

2. Second, train your staff in the art of selling as a matter of importance.

3. Third, have a financially rewarding incentive plan in place for staff when they do sell.

---

i See chapter... ◎ Get it done ♀ Thinking time ■ Example ☺ You can do it!

A Cause For More Sales...

One of the most common complaints that beauty industry staff have is that they are not paid enough. Most of the time this is due to the salon owners not being able to afford to pay their staff higher wages. Why? Because they rely to heavily on turnover from treatments. Whilst treatment sales will generate good revenue, the problem is, as you saw in the pricing of treatments, the costs associated with treatments are far more substantial than those associated with retailing a product.

Remember from chapter 5, Making Money; in the pricing of a treatment the main costs were wages, rent, stock used and the businesses overheads. With product sales, these costs are not included, hence the expected profit margins are much higher.

If you look at the most successful salon businesses around it becomes clear that retailing associated beauty products in your salon is a **key to success**. Look at:-

- HQ Hair - this brand have one small salon in central London and have a hugely successful online shop retailing absolutely everything to do with beauty!

- Nails Inc - selling their own brand of nail polish through a number of channels; online, teleshopping, nail bars, department stores.

- Bliss - selling their own brand of beauty treatments as well as other brands online, in stores and through a really cool catalogue.

- Toni&Guy - selling a range of haircare products through their franchised stores.

- The Cowshed - selling their branded products through their stores and in various department stores.

These are the more popular brands but there are others, individual shops that enjoy excellent returns because they focus on retail as much, if not more than, they do on treatments.

Address the financial concerns of your team by explaining that retailing in your salon equates to financial benefits to them... and mean it!

WHY SELL PRODUCTS?

Here *again* are the top reasons you must sell products in your salon:-

- Products have higher profit margins and therefore make more money than treatments.

- Faster form of revenue generation, i.e. make £10 in 1 minute from selling a product verses £10 in 15-20mins from providing a treatment! ...and as money is the aim of the game, you cannot deny this form of cash materialization!

- Provide your clients with the right products to keep their treatment going. Providing aftercare options is an important part of good customer service.

- Clients want to know what products you use on them and why they work. The fact that they are used professionally in a salon gives a product status and a feeling of quality. Clients like to have the option to buy these salon-grade products.

- A well merchandised salon looks good and can generate more business from passing trade! Entice passers-by to come in and browse, therefore increasing your footfall and hopefully your turnover.

HOW TO SELL PRODUCTS?

To create a salon that sells products effectively you will need to look at the following areas:-

- Correct product selection
- Effective presentation; Merchandising
- Testers
- Staff training
- Financially rewarding incentives

Correct Product Selection

It is vital that you choose the right products to sell in your salon. You will need to understand your market; their needs and spending power when making this choice. For instance, there is no point selling anti-wrinkle creams in a salon that specialises in funky nail art and body piercing; or selling expensive items if your location and clientele don't have a lot of disposable income.

Apart from selling the products you use for treatments there is also a whole host of other complementary products you can sell that you don't use. Great, affordable, everyday items to sell could be soft drinks, lip gloss, jewellery, hair accessories, snacks (apples, cupcakes) and so on.

■ **Example**
BLUEBERRY LOVELY® is a two room salon; the large main room has a 4-station manicure/pedicure bar, reception desk and café . The second room is much smaller but has an in-built shower room and is used for other treatments such as threading, waxing, massage, body scrubs, eyelash extensions, spray tanning, reflexology, facials, eyelash and eyebrow tinting, semi permanent makeup and Botox®.

All the products used in the salon are beautifully stacked on built-in shelves. I say 'stacked' and not 'displayed' because I want you to get a vision of a shop not a museum. I say 'beautifully' because I want you to get a vision of a well planned; colour, height, type and brand coordinated arrangement of products and not a market stand.

These shelves surround the seating in the café, they also face the clients sitting at the mani/pedi stations and are in the second treatment room. There are also cute bowls of quick-picks at the till.

The salons clientele are ladies who like to have tea (complimentary) or a smoothie (at a price), chat, have a pedicure, get their eyelashes enhanced and top-up on any other essential grooming. They have disposable income, like to meet their friends for coffee and like to look after themselves.

As such, also on sale in this salon are lip plumping lip-gloss, eyelash curlers, champagne, really pretty special pieces of custom jewellery, ghd hair straighteners, chocolate, pretty slippers (in case they forgot their open-toe shoes for after their pedicure), red shiny apples and more.

Passers-by come in just for the café which also doubles up as the salons waiting area. On the big communal table there are fashion magazines, product testers and fresh flowers.

This salon offers a variety of services and products and in doing so gives its clientele a fresh take on an urban day spa. It also enjoys a variety of revenue streams thus making at least double the amount of money a similar sized establishment would take that only offered treatments.

◎ Action
For your salon, try a series of different products and see which ones prove popular. A few attempts should help you become a *better buyer for your clientele.*

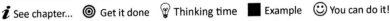

Effective Presentation; Merchandising

To merchandise is to promote the sale of goods especially by their presentation.

Merchandising is an art; presenting your products to maximum effect is something you should try again and again until you see that it's right. And even when you do get it right, keep updating the layout to keep it fresh and new to the eye.

◎ **Action**

- You should create easy to see-and-approach product displays;

- Put similar use products together;

- Have little info cards next to products; for instance, right next to your most popular cuticle oil or one of the most effective detangling shampoos, place a little information card giving browsers this important product information.

- Keep 'museum-style' product displays to a minimum; they are ineffective and just become part of the salons' decor; after a while your clients will switch off from actually seeing them!

- Take advantage of the different styles, colours and sizes of the packaging and place items in attractive combinations.

- As with a shop; try to create a layout that allows passers-by to feel that they can have an 'anonymous' visit to your salon/shop. Remember that people generally don't walk into a place like a salon just to have a look, because there is a feeling that once you walk in, you have made some sort of commitment! Occasionally, have a well positioned sign welcoming people to browse through the great products you have in your shop. Have 'open days' inviting passers-by to have a glass of wine, a sip of Pimms or an organic carrot juice and meet the team! Put attractive 'SALE' signs up when you have discounts on product lines.

Remember that well merchandised shelves should be able to sell themselves to some extent.

Keep thinking of innovative ways to attract people into your shop! ...once they are in, be friendly and helpful but not overwhelming!

Testers

Testers are also very important. Not all products can have a tester, shampoo for example, but many can, and you should make sure that potential buyers have free and easy access to the full range on offer.

Remember to keep testers reachable, presentable, clearly labelled and well organised.

Staff Training

So many employers just hand their team 'product information sheets' and expect them to get on with it and sell effectively. Whilst this may be enough information for an experienced or naturally talented sales person, it isn't enough for the majority.

This is because reeling off the features and benefits of a product to a client is not as effective as you may think it would be. It turns out that customers perceive and process your sales pitch or presentation in the following way:-

- 7% of the presentation is the actual content; i.e. what you are saying.
- 53% is your body language; i.e. the visuals and what they see in

you and the products packaging.
* 40% is the volume and tone of your voice.

It then becomes clear that just knowing and stating the features and benefits of a product isn't likely to sell the product as that is only 7% of what engages the customer.

It is true, there are some people who are just born sales people; that is partly because they are naturals at homing in on the key benefits of a product and letting that translate through their body language and tone of voice.

You and every member of your team can also be excellent sales people by creating a product-sales training programme covering the following:-

1. Product knowledge; features and benefits
2. First hand experience of the products
3. An open discussion amongst the team about the products
4. The importance of body language and tone of voice in selling
5. Role play
6. Effective selling techniques

The training can be done in 2 parts.

Part 1
Start by giving your team a clear understanding of why they need to sell products; the importance to the business and what benefits they will receive.

Then, go over every product on sale in the salon, especially the ones the team are most likely to use or be questioned about. Go over the key features and benefits of every product and give full product information sheets along with prices for your team to become familiar with. During and after this presentation, allow staff to try and test the products for themselves and experience the benefits first hand. They should all take away a few products to use until Part 2 of the programme. This type of understanding and buy-in of a product will go a long way in getting their body language and voice tone *naturally* attuned to a positive and enthusiastic presentation of the product.

Part 2
A few days later, get the team together and ask 2 or 3 of them to talk about something that is of interest to them. This can be anything from clothes to travel to relationships. Take note of their body language when talking about something they are passionate about. Then go on to discuss how they used the products and what they thought of them. Note the body language and tone of the people who liked the products. Discuss what effect their body language, volume and tone of their voice had on how interesting they were to listen to.

Follow this by doing a role play with all the team; some acting as customers, others as staff. Act out all the usual scenarios and have the best sales people show how they act and what they say to secure a sale.

Go on to round up the session by giving everyone a few extra selling techniques, like:-

- Build rapport with your client; find out things you may have in common and talk about them. This could be a favourite tv show, parenting, dieting, celebrities and so on.

- Try to recommend products before the treatment starts; maybe during a very brief initial consultation.

- Always recommend three products during a treatment;

- To close the sale, ask customers open ended questions, not ones that can be answered with a yes or no! For example, "Which one of these three product will you be taking home with you today madam?" instead of "Would you like to buy one of these products?"...NO!

Incentives

Obviously if you want your team to sell products you have to ensure that they know how and that their efforts will be rewarded. Incentives are briefly discussed in the Staffing, Making Money and Financial chapters of this handbook.

When pricing products, include the commission or amount per item you want to reward the seller.

Chapter 10
THE RECEPTION AREA
Customer relations begin at the front desk!

Customer relations begin at the front desk!

It is vital that you grasp the full importance and function of this area. Your receptionist can make or break your business; poor appointment bookings, poor communication skills both on the telephone and in person and poor organisational skills can cause a multitude of problems for your business; from missed revenue opportunities, to heaven forbid customer complaints!

THE RECEPTION AREA

Ensure the reception area is always manned or at least can be, very quickly. I suggest that you think of your salon as a 'shop with a till' that needs to be manned in order to take payments and not miss passing trade... think Boots, Superdrug or Walmart in terms of manned tills!

Next to the administration office of your business, the reception desk is the customer facing, centre of organisation of your salons day to day operations. This means that for a well functioning salon, the reception desk should be clean, very organised and its cupboards and surfaces well utilised.

Reception Area Functions:-

- Payment processing
- Appointment system, including booking-in, welcoming and checking-out clients
- Staff communications
- Customer communications
- Merchandising and retail

- Promotions
- Legal displays
- Waiting area

I will discuss each function separately.

Payment Processing
Your cash register and credit card processing machine should be on your reception desk. If you have a computerised appointment system, often these can be attached to the cash drawer so that you can 'close' a client's appointment by processing their payment through the computer. If your appointment system is not computerised then you should have a cash register or till at reception and programme it for all the different treatments and products your salon retails. Even the most basic tills have a way of distinguishing the different items that are processed through it.

Using your till or computer correctly to record transactions is a key part of keeping good financial records. Ensure that your team are properly trained to use the till and take payments. To minimise unauthorised or dishonest use of the till, only a chosen few should know how to make transactional corrections, refunds, etc when required.

My recommendation is to have a computerised appointment and payment system because the financial records that these systems generate can cut your accounting work load dramatically. However, they can be quite expensive and it may be wise to keep your capital expenditure to a minimum until your business has generated some profit.

Without a computerised system, I suggest you keep written records of the following in order to tally up your treatment appointments and other sales with the total in your till at the end of a trading day:-

- Customer appointments
- Therapist who did the work
- Total charge for treatment and any products sold by therapist

 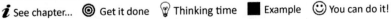

- Any stand alone product sales

These records will also be needed if you are paying your employees commission on sales. Remember the basics; you want to know what was done, by whom and for how much.

Appointment System

The appointment system is the way in which your clients are booked in for treatments from start to finish.

You may have a manual written system using an appointment book or a computerised system that keeps and consolidates therapist, client and sales records. For a manual written system you will need an appointment book or a diary. You can purchase ready made appointment books to suite your salon. Most beauty product distributors and stationers have a range of appointment books for sale.

An appointment system should include the following:-

- Greeting (telephone or in person).
- Booking a client in for treatment, including day, time, client name, telephone number, treatment, therapist name and any special considerations.
- Taking credit or debit card details to secure appointment (optional).
- If booking in person, offering an appointment reminder card (optional).
- If booking over the telephone, you could send a text to clients mobile with appointment details as a reminder (optional).
- Morning call to remind client and confirm appointment (optional).
- On arrival, welcome customer and mark appointment to show client has arrived.
- Inform therapist that their client has arrived.
- Have new clients complete a form.
- Once treatment complete, check to see that client knows how to maintain treatment results at home and take payment for any

products and treatment; mark appointment as complete.

- Book client for next appointment.
- Say your version of thank you and see you again!

Remember when booking in clients to account for lateness. However, a skilled receptionist can be creative, knowing the strengths and weaknesses of the team, she can ensure that the appointment book is as full as it can be!

Staff Communications

Staff communications include the following; the rota, cleaning or task rota, sales information and staff memos or notes.

For this I recommend that you purchase a clip board. Use your reception desk clip board to hold the latest rotas, task rotas, pay sheet log, individual sales log and staff memos/notes.

See *i* chapter 11, On-Going Management, for more details on these records.

Remember that rotas need to be near the appointment book or computer in order to facilitate quick and efficient appointment bookings.

Customer Communications

Communicating with your clients and passing trade is verbal, visual and written. Please see *i* chapter 13 on Marketing, for a more detailed look at this.

At reception, communication between your business and the client takes place on all levels and is the first point of contact for them. As such it needs to be welcoming, friendly and portray the brand image correctly and effectively.

Place the price list and other salon cards and promotional literature on your reception desk. Don't overload this area with too much information. Make sure to de-clutter regularly.

Have your salon telephone at reception. A cordless phone with an answering machine might be a good option if you don't have a full time receptionist. It's bad for business to not be able to answer the phone to clients trying to book appointments or ask questions. Make sure you respond to messages within the hour.

You can also use the reception desk to display any recent awards won by the salon or any of the team. Also, if you have had a flattering article written about you recently in a prominent publication, displaying this is a strong sales tool.

Merchandising and Retail

Merchandising and retail is covered more thoroughly in *i* chapter 9, Retail. However, in terms of merchandising on the reception desk, placing quick pick-up items next to the till can be very effective. For example, items under say £5 or £10 like handbag size nail oils, lip gloss, cute hand creams, face sun-creams or even a few luxury biscuits; these tend to sell really easily when clients are paying for treatments. Make sure your displays look appealing and easy to approach.

Promotions

Display any current promotions you have in the salon at reception. If you have limited reception space and you have a really good/ attractive offer on, then you may want to remove other regular reception items to give temporary space for this offer.

Legal Displays

Depending on your location, it may be a legal requirement for you to display your salons trading license and insurance. See *i* chapter 15 on H&S, Insurance and Licensing.

These one page documents are not central to your salons look, so as such I recommend you place them in clean frame-less Perspex frames on the wall near reception, keeping desk-clutter to a minimum. I also do not think that you should make a long (boring) display of all your staff's qualifications! I have seen these in some salons and it has done absolutely nothing to make me feel more confident in their abilities!

Waiting Area
If your salon has space for a waiting area this is a good place to make your clients feel welcome and to promote your business.

Ensure that your waiting area is always clean, tidy and fresh.

- If your business has a catalogue or brochure, display it here
- If your business has won any awards, display them here
- Display price lists and any other literature here also
- Try to position any seating in such a way to have clients facing a retail wall or shelf. Display products for sale.
- Display any promotional offers
- Offer up-to-date beauty, celebrity gossip and fashion magazines
- Offer waiting clients a drink; this is usually tea, coffee, water but you may also consider the more expensive option of wine and champagne (free of charge, otherwise you will need a license to sell alcohol!). You could sell other drinks like, fizzy drinks, smoothies and juices.

THE RECEPTIONIST - SALON COORDINATOR

Having covered the functions of a reception area you can see the importance of the receptionist's job. In fact, I don't think the job title, receptionist, accurately describes this crucial salon role! I see this role as quite a senior position and second to the role of salon manager. In my opinion the title of "Salon Co-ordinator" is more fitting as that is exactly what a person in this position will be doing; co-ordinating the day to day operations of the salon.

A salon co-ordinator works hand in hand with the manager and the rest of the team to see the smooth running of a busy salon.

She/he will need to know the days expected targets, chase up slow therapists, keep waiting customers happy, take important

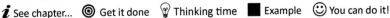

appointment details, know how to fill appointment book gaps; getting the most business for the salon, maintain client record cards, answer the phone, handle cash and cards, make add-on sales (this is a rare skill!), understand all the treatments; answering client queries correctly and keep smiling all the way!

The Salon Co-ordinator should be able to deal with people in a polite manner at all times, no matter how 'stressed' she/he may be, whilst questioning them to find out what they require and have the ability to also:-

- Welcome and receive people entering the salon
- Handle most enquiries efficiently
- Take and make appointments quickly; be able to recommend the correct treatments
- Deal with client payments
- Maintain the reception area

A great Salon Co-ordinator for a busy salon should have the following skills:-

- Excellent verbal communication
- Excellent listening ability
- Correct understanding of a situation/scenario
- Problem solving abilities
- Well organised
- Good memory
- Stamina
- Work very well under pressure
- Great people skills
- Excellent sales person
- A big smile and good looks!

A good salon coordinator could be your businesses greatest asset!

Chapter 11
ON-GOING MANAGEMENT
The day to day operations of your business

Staying in control of your business...

This chapter is about how to keep your salon running efficiently on a day to day basis; including your paperwork, monitoring staff performance, customer satisfaction and managing your finances.

THE ROTA

Rotas should be prepared at least 2 weeks in advance. This gives all employees the chance to plan ahead and let you know if they will have any trouble working the hours or days. Good practise would be to prepare a month's worth in pencil and ask the whole team to check and confirm their days. Once confirmed, finalise the rota by completing it in pen.

Being flexible in this way will help you run a salon with a mixture of part-time or full-time staff; some may be students, parents, etc, who may require some flexibility.

Flexibility is good but you will need to have some consistency, especially with your full-timers so that appointments can be made for weeks or months in advance, even if a rota doesn't yet exist.

In terms of staffing your salon well, try to ensure that you have the most staff in on your busiest days or during your busiest hours. This is also good if you offer a walk-in service.

■ **Example**
You may be open 7 days a week; Sun 9-5, Mon-Thurs 9-7 and Fri, Sat 9-8. Your busiest days are Fri and Sat and quietest days are Sun, Mon and Tues. You have a total of 5 staff; 2 part-time. Ideally you want at least 4 in on the Fri and Sat and a minimum of 2 on your quiet days.

Your rota could look like this:-

Staff	Sun	Mon	Tues	Wed	Thu	Fri	Sat
Angela	9 - 5	10 - 7	10 - 7	Off	Off	12 - 8	12 - 8
Tom	9 - 5	9 - 6	Off	Off	10 - 7	10 - 7	12 - 8
Sally	Off	Off	9 - 6	9 - 6	10 - 7	12 - 8	12 - 8
Carol	Off	Off	Off	10 - 7	Off	9 - 6	10 - 7
Charlie	Off	Off	Off	10 - 7	9 - 6	10 - 7	9 - 6
Totals	2	2	2	3	3	5	5

INDIVIDUAL SALES LOG

Keeping track of individual sales is very important for commission based wages and for monitoring individual and salon performance.

If you have a computerised appointment system or till then this log will be automatic and you will be able to run reports on individual staff sales for whatever period. If not then you will have to keep very good records throughout the day.

■ An example, of a sales log for Sunday is shown on the next page Note that the entries would be hand written as and when the payments are taken.

You might find it useful to create simple abbreviations for each treatment offered in your salon, like DCF for deep cleansing facial or FSA for a full set of acrylic nails, etc. This would save a lot of space on the log.

At the end of each day the sales log plus a cash register or till reading should be stapled to the rota that covers that day. At the end of a week you should have the week's rota plus seven sales log sheets and till readings for your records and calculations. You can keep 6 to 12 months worth of this weekly information in individual transparent sleeves in a large folder.

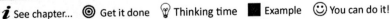

Angela	Tom	Sally	Carol	Char
Treatments				
Deep cleansing facial £30	Acrylic £60	Off	Off	Off
	Manicure £20			
Polish change £10	Manicure £20			
	Manicure £20			
Eyelash extensions £25	Pedicure £30			
	French polish £15			
Wax £40				
Total treatments £105	Total treatments £165			
Product Retail				
Face cream £30	Cuticle oil £10	Off	Off	Off
Face wash £7	Cuticle oil £10			
Enamel £9				
Cuticle oil £10				
Body cream £16				
Total retail £52	Total retail £20			
Total Sales £157	Total Sales £185			
TOTAL DAY SALES £342, SUNDAY 12th AUGUST				

The purpose of this exercise is to collect clear financial data of your business, which can be used to:-

- Calculate staff commission (if applicable).
- Calculate your % income if you are renting out salon space to a beauty professional.
- Assess individual staff performance.
- Provide income input for your cash flow and profit & loss calculations.

- Monitor stock usage and retail sales.
- Monitor what treatments are the most popular, what days are the busiest and what products are the best sellers.

Whether you collect this data via a computerised till or a hand written sheet, it is paramount for the successful management of your salon. Be aware that not computerising your reception can save you on your capital expenditure however, paperwork can be very detailed and time consuming. Weigh up the cost of you spending long hours doing your sums off the shop floor verses the cost of a computer system. Is it worth the initial saving?

Once you have decided upon the information you would like to see, create sheets to help you see this at a glance.

■ For example, I want to know what are the most popular treatments and products in my salon. It would be a long winded exercise to have to sift through sheets and sheets of daily sales logs. Instead I need to create a consolidated sheet of the relevant information. So for popular treatments and products analysis my sheet could look like this:-

Day	1	2	3	4	5	6	7	8	9	10	...etc	Total
Treatments												
Facials	10	4	2	8	3	2	4	5	7	12		**57**
Manicure	12	15	7	12	14	14	13	12	10	9		**118**
Wax	5	4	0	3	5	2	1	0	0	3		**23**
Pedicure	2	4	1	5	5	2	1	2	2	1		**25**
Tan	4	7	2	0	3	2	1	5	1	1		**26**
...etc												
Products												
Cuticle Oil	3	5	3	6	8	4	1	2	0	0		**32**
Face Cream	2	0	1	3	3	3	2	2	4	0		**20**
Body Buff	8	4	7	12*	14*	17*	7	7	2	3		**61**
...etc												

i See chapter...   ◎ Get it done   ♡ Thinking time   ■ Example   ☺ You can do it!

At the end of each day or week I can input all this information from my daily sales logs

I can now see that the most popular treatment in my salon is the manicure for which I charge £10 say and has therefore made the business £1,180 in revenue in 10 days. Now if I was planning a marketing campaign to make the pedicures or waxing more popular I would know to somehow link them to the manicures as I can see that most of my customers love to have manicures.

Also the promotion that I had going with the Body Buff for 3 days* really paid off as I can see sales of this product nearly doubled.

■ Another example
I am surprised to discover that we have run out of cuticle oil as I ordered 50 bottles just two weeks ago. I can take a quick look at my consolidated sheet and see that in 11 days we sold 34 of the 50, therefore there should be 16 left. It turns out that a whole box of 16 cuticle oils were dropped and broken without my knowledge. Not good, but at least not a mystery.

These are just a couple of examples of how a daily sales log can assist you manage your business effectively.

WAGES, PAY SHEETS AND COMMISSION

As with most salons, employees are usually paid an hourly rate and sometimes commission on sales.

Depending on how often you pay staff; weekly, bi-weekly or monthly, you should create pay sheets by combining the relevant information from the rota and the individual sales log to calculate wages.

A pay sheet could look like this:-

	Date	12th	13th	14th	15th	16th	17th	18th	Total
Angela	Hours	7	8	8	Off	Off	7	7	37
	Sales	£157.00	£185.00	£205.00	£0.00	£0.00	£256.00	£275.00	£1,078.00
Tom	Hours	7	8	Off	Off	8	8	7	38
	Sales	£185.00	£123.00	£0.00	£0.00	£198.00	£215.00	£310.00	£1,031.00
Sally	Hours	Off	Off	8	8	8	7	7	38
	Sales	£0.00	£0.00	£110.00	£130.00	£150.00	£30.00	£60.00	£480.00
TOTALS	Hours	14	16	16	8	16	22	21	113
	Sales	£342.00	£309.00	£315.00	£130.00	£348.00	£501.00	£645.00	£2,590.00

From this sheet you will be able to calculate the week's wages and any commission on sales. For instance, if you are paying Angela £7 per hour and 5% commission on all her sales, then her wages for the above week would be:-

37 hours x £7/hr = £259
5% of her £1079 sales = £53.95
Angela's total wages for the week are £259 + £53.95 = £312.95

Sally's wages for the week would be:-
38 hours x £7/hr = £266
5% of her £480 sales = £24
Sally's total wages for the week are £266 + £24 = £290

This pay sheet (as well as the daily sales logs) has highlighted the fact that Angela and Tom are by far more productive members of staff than Sally. Sally's wages are over half of her sales and in fact she is costing you money. Is she good for the business? What problems did she have on the 17th and 18th that caused her sales figures to be so low? Can you ensure that these problems don't occur again? If not then there may be a problem with keeping her in the business.

All of this information can be gathered and used during a staff performance review (see *i* chapter 7 on Staff).

Paying Your Staff

Your payroll company or accountant will give you forms to complete for each new member of staff. Once a person is set up on their system all you will have to do is send through their wages total so that they can process the pay.

Payroll companies do not need to know staff hours or sales totals, the only regular info you will need to send to them will be the individuals name along with their pay total and sick or maternity days.

For instance,
Ms Angela Smith £312.95

They will then send you her payslip and tell you how much to pay her after tax, or transfer payment to her on your behave.

MANAGING LATENESS

In my experience it's better to set penalties for excessive lateness rather than constantly have fruitless discussions with a team member who just can't seem to get to work on time! For example you may decide that 4 instances of lateness a month of 10 minutes or more (including late back from lunch) will incur a fine of £50. This way you will both have ample opportunity to figure out and resolve the cause of lateness however there will still be a consequence for excessive lateness if the employee continues to disregard their start times.

An easy way of keeping track of lateness would be to just put an "L" against the staff members name in the relevant day on the rota, and a double "LL" if late to work and late from lunch on the same day.

Count the number of L's at the end of each month. Don't forget to make sure that any penalties are clearly outlined in the staff handbook and each employee is aware of them.

CLEANING

If you are a busy salon it may be a good idea to hire a cleaner to do the general salon cleaning – wash rooms, showers, floors, walls, etc and to hire a salon junior to maintain work stations, the waiting area, etc during the day.
If this isn't possible be methodical and fair with the way cleaning jobs are distributed in your salon.

Creating A Task Rota

Rather than harping out instructions willy-nilly, using a task rota is a much better way of getting your team to participate in the maintenance of the salon. Displayed in the same way as the normal rota, a task rota will give each member of the team an area to clean or maintain during the week. Some tasks will be harder than others but if the task rota is rotated weekly, ensuring that everyone gets to do all the jobs, then at least this will seem fair.

It is really important to demonstrate exactly how each task should be completed. Remember that everyone has different standards of 'clean', so if you want things done to your standard then you will have to show what that actually means. When I opened my first salon, I assumed that my team would keep the brand-new, beautifully lacquered table tops that I had painstakingly designed as clean and polished as I would. This was not the case and I could never understand why. Once I had stopped getting upset about it, I realised that I hadn't actually shown anyone how I would clean the tops. You see, it's not that they didn't know how, but as they hadn't been instructed on exactly how it meant that technically they were free to 'cut corners'. After a demonstration however, anyone not completing a job correctly would be doing so knowingly and purposefully; this then takes on a very different meaning and should have consequences... read on.

You may also want to add a 'Task Free' row in the rota, allowing each person to have a task-free week or day regularly; this can be seen as a treat every once in a while, for example allowing that person to leave work earlier during those times.

To create a task rota you will need to know all the things that need doing regularly in the salon, these could be anything from refilling nail tip boxes or taking out the rubbish to mopping the floor at the end of the day. Make a list of the jobs and distribute them evenly and methodically over a 7 day period in the rota. If you are happy that all the jobs are covered correctly in your task rota then all you will need to do is rotate the staff names clockwise every week. Also it is very important to allocate ample time to get these jobs done; either by adding an extra 30 minutes to the end of a shift or during a quite time in the day.

The task rota also helps to highlight who is letting the team down and not completing their jobs properly. This should have consequences, like a loss of a task-free day or an open discussion with the whole team at a meeting, etc. Whatever you choose to do, there needs to be consequences as others will feel that they are not being treated fairly.

Waste Disposal

There are some treatments that are quite 'smelly' and waste needs to be contained until it can be disposed of at the end of the day. Acrylic liquid and acetone are examples of such smelly products. I think the best policy for any salon is to have metal, lidded pedal bins at every work station. All waste should be placed in these bins throughout the day, consolidated at the end of the day and disposed of in the outside bins for removal. This must be done everyday without fail.

In the UK, businesses pay the local councils waste disposal rates to have them collect their rubbish daily.

Work Station Organisation and Maintenance

Disorganised and dirty work stations not only put clients off but also:-

- Add precious time to a treatment due to operators searching for tools and products during a treatment
- De-motivate staff, who start to lose pride in their salon and work
- Create problems during stock counts and ordering, as it is unclear what's missing or required
- Cause risks to health, safety and hygiene and are ultimately a threat to the salons license, insurance and reputation

Cleaning and refilling work stations should be one of the tasks on the tasks rota. I have referred to these areas previously as Money Making Stations and as such they must be treated like your golden egg; maintained lovingly and thoroughly throughout the day.

Popping down to the stock room to refill a bottle of shampoo whilst your client is at the sink is just not on. Looking for a working nozzle for your resin whist in the middle of a full set of nails is just not on. It is paramount that any such issues are ironed out and procedures put in place to ensure a smooth running salon when it comes to equipment, tools and products for use during treatments.

FINANCIALS

Financial calculations are covered in detail in *i* chapter 14, Finance and Accounting. However, here I want to address the daily money matters that you will have to deal with either on the shop floor or as part of your back office administration work.

Setting Daily and Weekly Sales Targets

 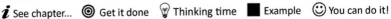

Setting realistic sales targets is an important staff motivation tool and a way for you to keep up-to-date with how your salon is doing financially.

Your weekly sales targets should come from your profit & loss estimates for the year. You can either divide your total expected revenue by 52 weeks (this is the number of weeks in a year) or you could be more season specific and divide each month's revenue by 4 weeks.

Once you have your weekly sales targets, divide this figure by the number of days you trade per week. You should also factor in that some days will be busier than others, so don't divide the week's target equally.

Once you have your daily sales targets, divide this up between all the staff who will be working on that day to give them all their individual sales targets for the day.

■ Example
Say the salons expected turnover for year 1 is £87,000.00

Calculating individual targets will be as follows:-

Weekly targets
£87,000 divided by 52 weeks in the year = £1,673.08 per week

Daily targets
£1,673.08 divided by 6 trading days a week = £278.85 per day

Individual targets
£278.85 divided by 3 staff = £92.95 per team member

You could at this point create a scenario for each therapist; highlighting the number of treatments plus sales that could help them meet their days target, e.g. Do 6 express manicures for £10 each, sell 3 bottles of cuticle oil for £11 each and achieve your target for the day! This helps the individual visualise how they can achieve their target;

turning what may seem like a boring sales figure into a practical comprehensible task. Remember that people think in different ways; this may not be necessary for all your team members, but it is your job to figure out what methods work for each individual.

Monthly Profit & Loss Records

At the end of every trading month you should feed in the actual sales and costs figures into the P&L you created in the original business plan. This exercise is very important! When you get to i chapter 14, Finances and Accounting, I will show you how to create a P&L forecast for the next 3 years of your business leaving a column empty next to each month for you to input the actual figures when you start trading.

■ **Example**
On the next page is an example of a P&L forecast for 3 years; the grey columns are empty for the salons actual trading figures as the business progresses through the years.

Paying Invoices

An invoice is another name for a bill; the difference is that it also acts as a receipt. When you pay for your meal at a restaurant, the waiter will present you with a bill and then after you've paid, give you a receipt. In the case of your business, a supplier will send you an invoice, either along with the goods or separately, clearly outlining the payment terms and accepted methods (i.e., exactly when and how they are expecting the money), but once paid they do not need to give you a receipt. The invoice will act as 'proof of payment' for your accounts and tax calculations. For this reason it is vital that you keep all your stock invoices and other receipts safe and organised. If you have delayed payment terms with your suppliers you will need to create a system that ensures you pay them on time. Beauty suppliers are not like the utilities suppliers for whom you

---

i See chapter... ◎ Get it done 💡 Thinking time ■ Example ☺ You can do it!

can delay bill payment. Most of the time they are small companies themselves and their cash flow has to be maintained to stay afloat. If a supplier feels that you are not a trusted customer they may stop supplying your salon.

Have an in-tray on your office desk; all outstanding tasks, including pending invoices should be kept here. You must be in the habit of looking through all the items in your in-tray every day. You could also buy a desk calendar; when an invoice arrives, mark out the day in the calendar for when you will need to send payment. Another way of keeping on top of invoices is to create a log sheet.

Profit & Loss Estimates
Year 1 - 3

Year	1		2		3	
Revenue	Forecast	Actual	Forecast	Actual	Forecast	Actual
Treatments	£91,800.00		£146,880.00		£165,240.00	
Retail	£9,180.00		£12,240.00		£18,360.00	
Online	£510.00		£6,120.00		£12,240.00	
TOTAL REVENUE	**£101,490.00**		**£165,240.00**		**£195,840.00**	
Direct Costs						
Rent	£15,000.00		£15,000.00		£15,000.00	
Wages (incl PAYE)	£35,190.00		£46,920.00		£58,956.00	
Employers NI Contributions	£2,463.30		£3,284.40		£4,126.92	
Stock	£14,280.00		£17,340.00		£20,400.00	
Licence	£700.00		£700.00		£700.00	
TOTAL DIRECT COSTS	**£ 67,633.30**		**£ 83,244.40**		**£ 99,182.92**	
GROSS PROFIT MARGIN	33%		50%		49%	
Indirect Costs/Overheads						
Accountant	£800.00		£800.00		£800.00	
Payroll company	£240.00		£300.00		£350.00	
Loan repayments	£1,440.00		£1,440.00		£1,440.00	
Advertising	£500.00		£500.00		£500.00	
Printing	£300.00		£300.00		£300.00	
Stationery	£300.00		£300.00		£300.00	
Phone / Utilities	£2,400.00		£2,400.00		£2,400.00	
Insurance	£720.00		£720.00		£720.00	
Legal services	£500.00		£500.00		£500.00	
Web site hosting & maintenance	£100.00		£100.00		£100.00	
Petty cash	£1,530.00		£1,530.00		£1,530.00	
Depriciation	£5,000.00		£5,000.00		£5,000.00	
TOTAL OVERHEADS	**£13,830.00**		**£13,890.00**		**£13,940.00**	
TOTAL COSTS	£81,463.30		£97,134.40		£113,122.92	
Miscellaneous costs @ 10% of total	£8,146.33		£9,713.44		£11,312.29	
PROFIT or LOSS	**£11,880.37**		**£58,392.16**		**£71,404.79**	
PROFIT MARGIN	12%		35%		36%	

Float

Float is a set amount of cash, always in the till, used for providing change to cash paying customers. Please ensure that you always have float in your till and that it is broken up into lots of change; it is really unprofessional when you are unable to provide your paying customer with the correct change quickly. Depending on how most of your clients prefer to pay; a decent float is around £40 to £100.

Cashing-up

Your till will come with instructions on how to zero it at the end of the day. Obviously this is something that should be done on a daily basis. So at the end of each trading day, count your cash, cheques and card transaction slips, tally these figures up with the till reading for the day and confirm that all is correct. Once completed, zero the till reading ready for the next day. Remember to not include your float in the days total and to leave it in the till.

I strongly recommend that you do not leave large amounts of cash in your shop overnight. You should get into the habit of banking money just before the banks close every day, that way the majority of cash and cheques wouldn't be in the shop overnight. If this is not possible then you must have a safe in which to store cash until the next bank run.

Petty Cash

Petty cash is cash that you will need to put aside for the inexpensive things that a salon may need to pay for regularly. For example, tea, coffee, water, sugar, milk, magazines, loo roll, washing-up liquid and so on. Keep an eye on this spending as it can sometimes get out of hand. Either budget an amount each week or have a little box by the till that contains a list of all cash taken from the till along

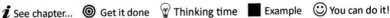

with receipts for all items purchased. This way you can tally up the spending at the end of each week. It should be made clear who has authorisation to take money out of the till; I think it should only ever be one person other than yourself.

Low Cash Flow!

Positive cash flow, as described in *i* chapter 14, is really the most important thing any business needs. Your business could be making profit but if there is not liquid cash available to pay your bills then there will be trouble.

How can a business be profitable and not have cash, I hear you ask? Well, say for example, every time your business makes some money you spend it on a new piece of equipment for the salon, you would have exchanged the cash for an asset. So your accounts will show profitability but there will be no cash for emergencies or bills.

I explain this in much more detail in *i* chapter 14.

Cash flow is about how well you manage your money day to day.

Your salons cash flow can be affected by the following:-

- Staff illness, absence or shortage; depending on the circumstances you may still have to pay wages even when they are not at work
- Time of year; January could have fewer customers than December for example
- Purchasing new equipment, furniture and tools
- Re-decorating
- Dealing with damage if uninsured
- Making high interest payments on loans and credit cards

- Having excessive amounts of stock in the salon that isn't shifting
- And ultimately, no customers!

If you are in trouble, then here are some cash flow fixes:-

- Try and sell off all excess stock at purchase price; may be on eBay (I have never tried this myself) or back to supplier
- Sell all your equipment and lease instead
- Contact suppliers and any other creditors, explaining your situation and make arrangements to pay later or over a longer period
- Get a temporary overdraft facility

 GOLDEN RULE - Make sure you can pay your staff wages, no matter what! Never allow your businesses financial matters affect their 'rice bowl'!

 *If your business is in trouble due to cash flow you must dig deep and bring out the fighting spirit that helped you start your business in the first place. Persevere, change your strategies and think of ways to solve your financial problems. Even the most successful business owners have had financial trouble before! Trust me!*

CUSTOMER SERVICE

The following topics all contribute towards providing your customers with the best service possible. Please read this section in conjunction with the next i chapter on Customer Service.

Salon Inspections

Salon inspections are an official way of regularly going over the functions, operations, cleanliness and organisation of the whole salon, marking the different categories out of 10.

Salon inspections should be carried out with an impartial eye; if you own and manage your salon as well, you may want to get someone else to do the inspection for you. That way you can get the real picture of how things look to others.

I have devised a full salon inspection sheet with 10 questions that cover everything from the salons' appearance, to organisation, to staff participation. It is available to purchase from www.misssalonbusiness.com for £3.99 and you can use it in your salon.

I recommend that a salon inspection is carried out at least once every two months.

Mystery Shoppers

A mystery shopper is someone who contacts and uses the salon as though they are a customer, however, taking note of their entire experience for your records.

Mystery shoppers are especially useful when you are not on the shop floor and unable to see things for yourself. They are a way for you to monitor the quality of the customer care that your staff provide.

When seeking someone to do this for you, ensure that they are unknown to the team and have the necessary communication and writing skills to report on their visit clearly and objectively. All their treatments should be free in return for this report.

A mystery shopper should complete a questionnaire after their visit, covering the following areas:-

1. The booking process
2. Their welcome into the salon
3. What their first impressions were
4. The quality of the service
5. Staff engagement during their visit
6. Their comfort levels
7. The aftercare offer; retail
8. Their overall thoughts on whether the visit was value for money
9. Would they come back?
10. Would they recommend the salon to their friends?

When acting upon the feedback given, do this in a fair and controlled way. If the feedback was particularly negative about a certain member of staff then this person should be approached and the issues discussed in a formal and private way. If feedback was negative about the salon in general then a staff meeting would probably be the best arena for a solution-finding discussion. If feedback was positive, then give lots of praise!

Maintaining Client Records

I know this all sounds obvious but I must say that client records, whether computerised or hand written, almost always get disorganised, doubled-up and out-of-date if there isn't a strict process by which they are handled. All too often client names are misspelt and duplicate records created, or client names are entered in lowercase causing problems when printing communications, or

i See chapter... ◎ Get it done ♀ Thinking time ■ Example ☺ You can do it!

post codes are wrong, last visits not entered and so on.

Good practise would be to check them once a month. Also, your team need to be trained on how to either, input and update client info on the computer, or, create and update client record cards. They should be taught to understand the importance of these records.

The proper maintenance of client records is an important part of salon management for the following reasons:-

- Complying with the Data Protection Act
- Health & Safety of clients
- Complying with the salons licensing requirements
- Marketing
- The long-term valuation of the business

Data Protection Act
In the UK, client records are protected and governed by the Data Protection Act 1998. See what your business must do in order to comply with this act in *i* chapter 13 on Marketing.

Health & Safety and Licensing
It is a health & safety and therefore licensing requirement to keep minimum information on all clients. There are some spa and salon treatments that require you to have a good understanding of a person's medical history, whether they are taking any medication, their diet, some aspects of their lifestyle and their general health. These client records can be quite detailed but absolutely vital before treatment. Make sure that you have client record cards/ spa registration questionnaires designed to collect all the vital data before performing specialist treatments. Also see *i* chapter 15 on H&S, Licensing and Insurance.

Marketing
Well maintained client records will help you contact your customers with relevant offers, events and promotions. See *i* chapter 13 on Marketing.

Valuation of the business
Your client records are one of the things that add value to your business. If, for example, you think of selling your salon, access to the clients that come with the business will be one of its most valuable assets.

Regular Clients

Regular clients are a sign of a healthy salon business. If your customers are coming back to you, then you must be doing something right! It also suggests that your client list is likely to keep growing.

Your well maintained client records will highlight whether or not this is happening for you. If not then you must address the problems pronto, as your business will not last long. To help you pinpoint what could be going wrong, do a salon inspection and get a few mystery shopper reports.

Regulars must be acknowledged and rewarded. Use your client records to note details about the client that can be used to make them feel more welcome, comfortable and valued at every visit. For example, remember their name, the way they like their coffee, the last treatment they had and their beauty goals. Reward regulars with special discounts, previews and first picks. Ensure that they can get the appointment slots that they need; to avoid disappointment, advise them in advance if they need to book early during a particularly busy period.

Also, it is important to make sure that the clients are coming back to the salon not only because they 'love' their therapist, hairdresser or nail technician, but also because they 'love' and trust the salon. This is important as staff will come and go but your business should remain!

PROMOTIONS

Regular promotions are a necessary part of marketing your salon. Promotions help to attract new customers and keep regulars engaged with the salons' activities, not just on their usual treatments. Promotions and how they should be created are discussed in chapter 13 on Marketing, however here I will talk about the management process of a promotion.

After deciding on a particular promotion, educating your team on the details of that promotion is vital to its success. A staff meeting is the best arena for this.

Secondly, creating a system whereby you can measure the success rate of the promotion is also key to creating successful promotions in the future. For instance, you should want to know how many new customers you attracted to your salon through a particular offer.

Keep a log of all promotions; noting uptake numbers and whether it was a success or not.

REPAIRS

Equipment

Your salon equipment must always be in working order; for both Health & Safety and efficiency reasons.

From sun beds to desk lamps, when these items are being installed note their warranty information and whether the suppliers offer a repair service. Keep a log of all equipment and the repair service contact details. Also keep contact details of your electrician, plumber, carpenter and shop-fitter.

As soon as something's not working right, fix it.

Signage

There is nothing less welcoming or more unattractive than a dirty or broken sign! A letter missing or a dead light bulb portrays a terrible image. Keep your businesses exterior display in tip top condition. Have the signage company's contact details at hand so that these sorts of repairs can be handled quickly and with minimum fuss.

YEARLY RENEWALS

There are documents that will need renewing once a year; these include your insurance policies, salon license and your business plan. You will receive automatic reminders for the insurance and license renewals. The business plan, however, is in your hands and requires you to be diligent enough to ensure that you check how your business is doing against the plan.

PAPERWORK

Being organised with your paperwork is one of the keys to success. Try to keep your office desk up-to-date and clutter free. Create a system, a daily routine with paperwork that works for you. Remember that a lot of the daily salon paperwork can be done and kept at the reception desk (see *i* chapter 10, Reception Area). Other, more detailed jobs like, profit and loss analysis, performance reviews and cash flow updates shouldn't be done on the shop floor. Use your lockable filing cabinet to store salon and staff information, this includes items like till cashing-up receipts, staff files, bank statements, company registration document or partnership arrangements, original insurance and license docs, etc. Please note that staff are entitled to have access to their records at any time, however, it is still your duty to keep their information private.

Paid invoices and receipts should be consolidated by month and type

---

and kept in a box folder marked 'Accountant'. You should have an agreement with your accountant as to how often you send through these documents.

You will also need to create folders to house sales logs, past rotas, salon inspection sheets, profit and loss records, customer complaints, accident reports, etc.

UK law requires businesses to keep all their records for at least five years and ten months after the end of the tax year the records relate to.

If you are a naturally organised person, creating a record-keeping system will be quite straight forward for you. However if you could do with some more ideas on how to go about this then I recommend you have a look at the following web page:-

Business Link **www.businesslink.gov.uk**
Select 'Tax, returns & payroll', then under 'Legal structures, records & returns', select' Administration, records and reporting'. You will then have the option to read more about how to 'Set up a basic record-keeping system'

Chapter Summary

Managing your salon and business operations is about being organised and having good time management skills. Take some time, before you open the salon, to think about how you plan to run the business day to day. Create you logs and sheets to record daily activities which can be consolidated and used to calculate wages, P&L accounts, popular treatments and much more.

Chapter 12
CUSTOMER SERVICE

Treat your customer expertly, respectfully & empathically

Satisfied customers should be every salons dream!

WHAT IS GOOD CUSTOMER SERVICE?

Think of your salon as your home; if a not-so-familiar guest arrives to your house how would you welcome and host them? What about if you went to visit a friend in their home; how would you expect to be treated? I certainly would expect a minimum of:-

The Welcome...

A "Hello" with a warm smile
A nice comment on how I look or a question about how I am
An offer to take my coat, or where I should leave my bag
An indication of where I should head towards
A suggestion to relax and take a seat
An offer of a drink or some refreshment

Attention and Interest...

After this 'welcome' I would expect my host to be interested in speaking to me and hope that they would be able to stop any other activity to spend some quality time with me. If their phone rings I would hope that they would excuse themselves and apologise for the interruption. If they needed to leave the room for any reason, they would let me know and hurry to get back to me, their guest.

Basically, I would hope to feel that my visit was welcome and valued.

The Exit...

On leaving I would hope to be escorted to the door, thanked for visiting, asked if I had a good time, to visit again and bid farewell.

The above, I would say, are the very basics of being a good host. And this is the very minimum that should be offered to a customer in your salon. Even if my guest arrived slightly flustered, or irritable, or late, or even didn't behave all that well, I would be principled and naturally still behave in the same manner... They, however, might not get a second invite!

Many would say that this is obvious; that they know this is what they need to do for every customer, but be sure that there is a big difference between knowing what to do and actually doing it... no matter what. Salon staff can become complacent, bored, arrogant, tired, forgetting their manners and ethics. This happens very often. Staff must be trained in customer service techniques, have regular reminders and perhaps rewarded for outstanding service.

◎ Teach your team that every customer should be welcomed, seen to with skill, enthusiasm and attention and finally bid farewell. Remember that this is a relationship that you are trying to start and nurture for continued mutual benefit.

GOOD CUSTOMER SERVICE AND THE BEAUTY PROFESSIONAL

Be professional... what does that mean? So many people say that but I don't think it is always clear what being professional actually means. A professional is somebody who shows a high degree of skill or competence and whose occupation requires extensive education or specialized training. That is the meaning of a professional in terms of the actual job but what about being a professional in terms of customer service...

i See chapter...   ◎ Get it done   ♀ Thinking time   ■ Example   ☺ You can do it!

A professional that is client-facing has to have a specific set of skills and a real commitment to the job in order to always be able to provide an excellent all-round service.

Every member of the salon team is responsible for ensuring that they do all they can to provide anyone in the salon with the best experience from start to finish.

Providing the best customer service requires a beauty professional to:-

- Have a clear understanding of and commitment to their job, like arriving to work on time, keeping up with the task rota and so on.
- Understand that any negative behaviour from them not only reflects badly on themselves but also the salon as a whole.
- Be in a good mood and have a positive attitude.
- Have the ability to empathise with a customer's needs.
- Be a good listener.
- Admit when they have made a mistake and be able to apologise.
- Be friendly but not overwhelmingly so or too personal. Ask questions but don't pry.
- Have good manners.
- Be a people person.

These skills will go a long way in helping an individual provide the type of quality service that is unfortunately lacking in a lot of salons.

◎ Make sure your business stands out in this area and shines through as the best place to spend ones precious time and hard-earned cash!

Don't be the salon caught-out with bored, lazy-looking, gum-chewing front of house staff!

Help! A Difficult Client!

These days most of us live in a stressed-out world; money issues, time issues, etc. There are all kinds of reasons why a customer could walk into your salon with a bit of a negative aura around them. For all you know she just got a parking ticket, her wedding flower arranger has let her down, her boyfriend's upset her or she's just feeling a little tired! A person in this position may not make the best first impression on you when they walk in, but you as the service provider, the host, the professional on stage, always have the opportunity to not react to their approach but to pro-actively provide your best service ever.

I have witnessed nail bar staff, for example, being abrupt and quite unhelpful to clients that seem to have an 'attitude'. Who wins? Who loses? I think it is a loss all-round. Loss of business principles, loss of dignity and a loss of a growth opportunity! Most "difficult" customers, if handled skilfully and empathically will probably become your most loyal clients; always remembering the way in which you did such a good job with their hair and made their day that bit better!

Handling Customer Complaints

You should consider having a Customer Complaints Policy in place from the start. When a customer actually takes the time and musters up the courage to complain it means that they really feel let down by some aspect of your service. You would want to know that this person is taken care of efficiently and with the best possible outcome every time! A Customer Complaints Policy can help to regulate this.

If the business consists of one salon, and you the owner, are on site most of the time, then you could have a discretionary attitude to how complaints are dealt with. I was always quite horrified to have a client come back unhappy with their treatment and immediately, without question or discussion offered to give them the full treatment again, with another member of staff. Depending on how wrong the first treatment was I may have gone on to offer further subsequent

i See chapter... ◎ Get it done ♡ Thinking time ■ Example ☺ You can do it!

treatments free of charge or half price. The aim of this was to restore their confidence in our salons service and ensure that their tales about the salon would still have a positive tone.

Remember, word of mouth is king!

I advise following the below steps when handling a complaint and maybe producing your Customer Complaints Policy from these steps:-

- Listen to the problem
- Immediately apologise for their upset
- Investigate and log the problem
- Compensate the client
- Deal with the root cause

Listen and apologise

Whether you think you know what happened or not, whether you think they are right or wrong, you must always give the client the opportunity to tell their story and apologise for the fact that they are unhappy (not necessarily for the cause of their unhappiness). Once you have reasonably established what happened and you think that the salon could have done a better job then definitely apologise for the salons/therapists errors and promise to rectify and compensate.

Try and make sure that complaints are handled discretely. Don't allow things to get out of hand on the shop floor, in front of other clients. If a customer is hell-bent on making a scene then I think you should weigh up the value of just giving them a full refund or having them frighten other clients!.. I would apologise for their upset, give them a refund and bid them farewell... and deal with the cause later!

Investigate and log the complaint

99% of the time, the client has a case for complaining and should be compensated before your full investigation and log. Remember the customers needs come first in these matters. If however, you think that some investigation is required before offering a solution to the client then be sure to explain that to them. You could say something along the lines of, "Your business is important to us and I am so sorry that you are unhappy with our service, please allow me the opportunity to investigate this matter thoroughly and contact you within the next day to offer a solution"

Investigating the matter should include talking to the member of staff who performed the treatment and any other staff members who may have witnessed the service or were present that day.

Log the complaint as follows:-

1. Date of complaint
2. Date of treatment
3. Client name
4. Therapist name
5. Customer's complaint
6. Therapist's version of events
7. Your comments
8. Compensation offered
9. Client's response
10. What's been done to ensure this doesn't happen again

Compensate the client
You could offer repeat treatments, treatment packages or partial refunds depending on the issue. I believe that full refunds are a last resort. A full refund will almost likely mean you will never get their business again. Remember you are aiming to keep the customer, not get rid of them, offering a repeat treatment will allow you to get it right second time and to show that your salon is still a good place for them to visit.

Deal with the root cause
There is no point going through all of the above if you are not going to ensure that it doesn't happen again! Customer complaints are a costly business, not only in terms of actual cash or salon time but also in terms if reputation. Your businesses reputation is very important

to its growth and on-going success.

Your investigation should have highlighted the cause of the problem in the first place. It could have been due to a stressed out employee; maybe over worked and undervalued or in the wrong job. It could have been due to poor equipment or poor handling of equipment. It could have been that the employee does not know how to give a certain treatment. Or a whole host of other reasons. Whatever the case maybe, take your time to plan and execute a solution to the root cause of any complaint.

◎ It is important to bear in mind that this exercise is not about who to blame but how to not have it happen again. Be sure not to instigate a blame-culture in your salon; you want your team to look out for each other!

GOOD CUSTOMER SERVICE AND THE SALON

The previous topic was about how a beauty professional affects good customer service. In this section I want to show how the salon as a whole plays a part in good customer service.

A salon providing the best customer service:-

- Is clean, tidy and has high standards of hygiene
- Provides clean and properly functioning facilities; toilets, showers, etc
- Is Health & Safety conscious, including, holds the correct insurance, has a proper risk assessment, uses properly working equipment, is well lit and properly ventilated
- Offers appropriately priced and well executed treatments
- Displays a clear price list
- Offers a full range of aftercare products
- Has well trained and helpful staff
- Remembers and rewards regular clients

Customer Service When Business Is Really Good

Don't allow yourself and your staff to become complacent and arrogant. This can easily happen when business is good, the salon is busy busy busy and you think you can afford to miss new business. You think you can afford to not take the time with that difficult customer... well, you can't. Always remember to think of the 'lean' times; always treat every customer like gold dust!

CUSTOMER SATISFACTION

A full appointment book and a growing number of regular clients is an obvious indicator of customer satisfaction. But what if your not there yet; how do you know if your salon is doing a good job for its customers?

Setting **customer service targets** will help to keep track of your customer's satisfaction and keep your staff motivated.

Methods of Measure

There is no specific way to do this; you can tailor your methods of setting salon/staff targets according to your specific business. Get thinking 💡 !

Here are some examples of how you could measure customer satisfaction:-

- You could monitor how many return customers are generated per month and by which therapist.

- You could also have a series of mystery shoppers report on their salon experiences.

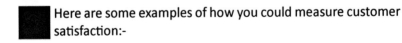

- You could ask all customers, at reception, to give anonymous feedback by ticking a 4 question card after every treatment:-

  1. Are you happy with your treatment?
     ☐ YES   ☐ NO   ☐ NOT SURE

  2. Do you feel you got value for money?
     ☐ YES   ☐ NO   ☐ NOT SURE

  3. Would you recommend this salon to your friends?
     ☐ YES   ☐ NO   ☐ NOT SURE   ☐ MAY-BE

  4. Would you recommend your therapist to your friends?
     ☐ YES   ☐ NO   ☐ NOT SURE   ☐ MAY-BE

Consolidate the results to get a general view of what your clients think of your business.

*With customer service, remember the obvious...
no customers, no business!*

Be nice to your guests... Be the best!

Chapter 13
MARKETING
Reach and keep your customers

Packaging, presenting, promoting, advertising, selling!

WHAT IS MARKETING?

The dictionary definition of Marketing is "the business activity of presenting products or services to potential customers in such a way as to make them eager to buy".

The business activity... that means all the areas of the business required to present the "product to the market". Areas like the location, the name, the colours, the advert, the furniture, the leaflets, the welcome, the layout, the treatments, the products and so on. All these play an important role in presenting your product to the market.

In a nutshell, Marketing is about attracting customers, getting them to choose your product or service and keeping them coming back for more!

Make no mistake, having a marketing strategy and plan is the most important thing you can do for your business.

MARKET RESEARCH TIPS AND METHODS

As an aspiring entrepreneur you need to develop your unique idea, construct a market analysis, assess the competition, create a sales and marketing plan, determine risks and rewards and then execute your plan.

Let's face it, opening a salon is not a unique idea but how you package it can be quite unique. However, even if your packaging is not unique but the location and therefore target market is calling for a hairdresser or a masseuse or a skin rejuvenation specialist then you're likely to succeed because you will be fulfilling a need. Either way, in order to create a relevant business and actually fulfil a need you will have to construct a market analysis, ultimately aiming to identify a particular group of people who need something that you can provide.

But how do you do this? Well, generally, in the first instance you go by your own needs and instincts. I started my first nail bar because I struggled to find a good salon to get my own nails done. However, before I could be sure that it would be a viable business I had to do some in-depth research to confirm that I wasn't the only one who wanted my nails done!

There are 2 types of market research:-

1. Quantitative; how many people want it, do it, like it, etc?
2. Qualitative; how do they feel about it, why do they want it, why do they like it, etc?

You can do your own research, pay a company to do it for you or buy already prepared market reports.

For the purpose of your first salon I would recommend you do your own research. Firstly it's free(ish). Secondly as your business reach is limited to the locality of the salon the scope of your research is manageable and therefore physically possible for you to conduct; alone or with friends. Thirdly, you need to observe, know and hopefully meet your target market and competitors face to face; you are the best person for this job!

If you would prefer to pay for data or feel uncomfortable or unable to do the research yourself then you can find and hire many professional research companies online. Just beware; they are not cheap!

Buying already prepared market reports can be even more expensive, however if you can afford it they can be very useful.

For example there is a report available to purchase on www. mindbranch.com called The Professional Beauty Market UK 2006 for $2,968.00! I have not personally read this report, so I cannot recommend it, but it sounds good.

I still recommend DIY!

Market Research Methods; Data Collection:-

- Interviewing individuals*
- Creating a simple questionnaire
- Conducting relevant group discussions
- Performing treatment and/or product tests
- Observing an area
- Visiting competitors

* Please note; carrying out street interviews requires local authority licensing

Use the above data collection methods to identify and quantify your target market. What you actually need to know about these potential customers is discussed in more detail in the following sections. **But before this, here is a simple example of market research and how the results can be used in your business plan:-**

Example
The business idea is an eyebrow grooming bar on a busy high street. The target market is definitely female. Using the 'simple questionnaire' and 'visiting competitors' method, I decide to do some field research and collect data to:-

- Identify what type of woman is likely to visit the bar;
- Estimate how many of these women there are in the local area;
- Find out how much they are willing to pay;
- Have some information about their grooming choices

I created a simple questionnaire, asking the following:-

1. Are you...

☐ Female
☐ Male

2. Are you...

☐ Married
☐ Single
☐ Living with partner

3. Do you...

☐ Have children
☐ Not have children

4. Are you...

☐ Employed
☐ Unemployed
☐ A student
☐ Self-employed

5. What age group are you in?

☐ 18-25   ☐ 26-35   ☐ 36-45   ☐ 46-55

6. Do you go to a salon to have all or any of the following done:-

☐ Hair
☐ Nails
☐ Tan
☐ Eyebrow shaping / tint, eyelash tint / extensions
☐ Facials or body treatments

---

i See chapter...   ◎ Get it done   ♀ Thinking time   ■ Example   ☺ You can do it!

7. Do you pluck, wax, thread or shave your eyebrows?

☐ Pluck ☐ Wax ☐ Thread ☐ Shave
☐ I don't shape my eyebrows at all (please go to question 9)

8. Who shapes your eyebrows...?

☐ I do them myself
☐ A friend does them for me
☐ I go to a salon / beautician

9. Do you want to / like to have your eyebrows done?

☐ Yes ☐ No (please go to question 12)

10. Would you like to go to a salon to get your eyebrows done? Do you like getting your eyebrows done in a salon?

☐ Yes ☐ No (please go to question 13) ☐ Not sure

11. How much do you or would you pay for eyebrow shaping?

☐ £5 - £10
☐ £11 - £15
☐ £16 - £25

12. Why do you not want someone else to shape your eyebrows?

☐ (A) I like my eyebrows the way they are
☐ (B) I do them well enough myself
☐ (C) I am afraid to have them shaped
☐ (D) I don't think this is important
☐ (E) Never thought about it
☐ (F) Can't afford it
☐ (G) None of the above

13. Why would you not like to go to a salon to get your eyebrows done?

☐ (A) Don't know a salon that offers this service
☐ (B) I do them well enough myself
☐ (C) Don't trust anyone to do them for me
☐ (D) I don't think this is important
☐ (E) Never thought about this
☐ (F) Can't afford it
☐ (G) None of the above

Analysis and Conclusions From This Example Questionnaire

- Questions 1 to 5 tell me about the type of female.
- Questions 6 to 8 are about their grooming choices, useful for future marketing activities.
- Questions 5 and 7 tell me whether they already go somewhere for this service.
- Questions 9 to 13 tell me about the best price point and help to estimate the number of potential customers.

Say I managed to get 100 women to complete the questionnaire on or near the high street of interest with the following results...

1. I have estimated that I might expect the following number of customers:-

   All those who answered question 11 (17 responses)
   All 'not sure' answers to question 10 (0 responses)
   All who answered B, C or E to question 12 (8 responses)
   All who answered A, B or E to question 13 (12 responses)

   This totals **37** potential customers out of 100

i See chapter... ◎ Get it done ♀ Thinking time ■ Example ☺ You can do it!

2. I have estimated how much they are willing to pay from the most popular answer to question 11:-

This was the **£5 to £10** option

3. I have identified the most popular type of customer from counting the answers to questions 1 to 5 against those of 10 to 13 as explained above.

This equalled mostly **single or living with partner; no children, employed and aged between 26 -35.**

So For My Business Plan, I would conclude...

My potential market is 37% of the adult female population within a certain postcode (area code). Say that population is 8,100 women; my potential market is equivalent to 37% of 8100 ≈ 3000 women. Of course these figures must be taken with a pinch of salt; after all, I only spoke to 100 women! There are so many other factors that could be considered but on the whole this information can give you some foundation for your financial forecasts and marketing strategies. I would suggest that you reduce the percentage by 10; so 27% of 8100 ≈ 2000 women.

From question 11, I see that 17% already pay for or would be willing to pay for the service, this is approximately 1300 women. Is this enough? In my financial forecasts, as described in chapter 14, I would do well to base my future revenue estimates on getting just 10% of those women to regularly visit the threading bar. That is 130 women every month spending an average of £8 ≈ £1000 a month revenue. Is this enough? The answers to question 6 tell me what other services may be important to add in order to try and increase the turnover.

Visiting and studying competitors has also given me some extra information. For instance, most local salons are charging £10 to £15 for eyebrow shaping.

Summary conclusions for my business and marketing plan:-

- The market size for the threading bar in a specific postcode area is approximately 2000; however there may be more potential customers in other local areas.

- I should base my initial forecasts on approximately 130 customers a month

- I should consider charging more than £8 for the service

- I should look into providing other services to boost income

- I can specifically target a certain type of woman in my advertising and promotional campaigns

Remember this was an example, designed to help you figure out how best to identify, quantify and qualify your target market. Take time to plan the best market research method for your business.

More Tips...

A great way to get people to stop and talk to you is by offering them something nice... Chocolate can work wonders! Invest £50 in a huge sack of popular chocolates and make a sign or t-shirts that says something like "A chocolate bar for 2 minutes of your time!" Prepare 6 clipboards with pens and questionnaires and have you plus two of your attractive friends try and get people who look like your target market (in the right location) to stop and fill in the questionnaire! Try and pick a sunny day and a time when people are not in a hurry to get home or to work; may be a Saturday afternoon or a bank holiday.

Another tip...

You can get populations of any borough in the UK from www. statistics.gov.uk ⇨ Select the 'Neighbourhood' option and then type in the postcode and select 'Ward' as the type of area you need stats for.

For the USA this information can be found on www.census.gov

CREATING A MARKETING PLAN

A marketing plan is the route you will use to reach your target audience.

Having done your market research and analysis, create your marketing plan as follows:-

1. Identify your target market and therefore where your business needs to be located.

2. Based on your market research define and price your product and service offer, including your unique selling point.

3. Set a marketing budget; the maximum amount you can spend on getting your salon noticed!

4. Give your product and service an image, a brand.

5. Plan your launch, promotional and advertising campaigns, including setting sales and marketing targets.

6. Sell your product and service.

7. Have a contingency plan if you don't hit your targets.

Let's look at all of these sections individually...

1. Identify Your Target Market & Best Location

First, define your target audience and highlight their need for your product. Who will visit your salon? Who are you opening your salon for? Why will they visit your salon? Please stay away from the view that is so common amongst new business owners who just imagine everyone is their customer! **Everyone is not your customer.** If you think in that way you will never know what specific things you can do for your business to get the punters in. As explained in 'The Market' section of the Business Plan, *i* chapter 3 and in the above market research example; define your customer by gender, age, location, interests, occupation and income bracket. Also define their needs in terms of beauty aspirations, personal maintenance and what their preferred relaxation/de-stressing methods are.

◎ As an exercise, have a look at and think about the target market of some of these salons (UK):-

- **The Hay Barn** located in the country
  (www.daylesfordorganic.com, select 'The Hay Barn')

- **Bliss** located in Kensington, London
  (www.blisslondon.co.uk)

- **Inner Sanctuary Spa** in the City Centre, Manchester
  (www.innersanctuaryspa.com)

- **Elizabeth Arden Red Door Spa** located in Mayfair, London
  (www.reddoorspas.com)

- **Bloww** located in Soho, London (www.bloww.com)

Choosing A Location
Now that you know who you are trying to target you should also know the areas where the highest number of them live, work and play. ◎ Plan your premises searches around these locations.

i See chapter...   ◎ Get it done   ☿ Thinking time   ■ Example   ☺ You can do it!

2. Define Your Product, Service & Unique Selling Point

Once you are clear about who you are targeting, move on to clearly defining your product and service for that audience. What is your offer? Is it a fast manicure and pedicure service, or a tanning shop, or a specialist beauty treatment salon offering electrolysis, Botox® and skin peels? Whatever your products and services are, list them here.

You will need to price these products and services based on your target market's spending power, the salons location and your business costs. You would have already seen in *i* chapter 5, Making Money, how to price individual treatments and products based on your business costs; now you need to look at those prices and see that they are in line with all your other marketing efforts.

Branding your offer comes next. The section below on branding will help you do this for your business. Branding your business, product and service will include naming it, packaging it, giving it a personality, a colour scheme, a slogan and so on.

With a branded product you are then ready to present, promote and sell it!

USP (Unique Selling Point)

What is your USP? What makes you different from the other salons around you? Are you appealing to the young, hip crowd, or a mainly male clientele? Will your organic product range, or black walls and dark furniture, or open-plan layout, or no-noise policy make you standout and particularly appeal to your market?

◎ Make sure there is something that is obviously unique about your business that is of particular interest to your target market.

3. Set A Marketing Budget

Your marketing budget will be used to pay for things like your logo design, leaflets, press packs, pricelists and banners. It can also cover any advertising, launch day parties, special promotional freebies or maybe even hiring a PR agency.

I think it wise to not spend too much on any one part of the plan. Do as much as you can on your own and pay for the things you really can't do without. When you discover what works, ultimately meaning customers through the door and money in the till, then you can concentrate more of the budget in that area.

For example don't spend loads on a newspaper or magazine advert just stating the facts about your new salon; it might be ineffective, especially if there are loads of salons around. You may be better off spending the money on a launch party or advertising the party.
Just like budgeting for your shop fit and having to be creative when you can't afford a particular piece of furniture or wall display, you will need to be tight with your marketing budget, spending wisely and improvising wherever you can.

4. Branding

What is a brand? A brand is a symbol or a name that embodies all of the information connected to your business which serves to create associations and expectations around it. You would aim to ensure that these associations and expectations are positive and create a feeling of trust towards your business.

A brand can be composed of the following elements:-

*   Functionality; what the brand claims and can deliver
*   Personality; its lifestyle and values
*   Its relationship with the client

Functionality
What is your brand claiming it can do? You could be offering your

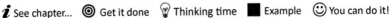

clients the best tan in town, or the most natural looking nails, or a quiet and pleasurable experience. You could be adamant that only the most experienced and competent people are employed in your salons, therefore almost guaranteeing your clients the best results every time.

Personality

Expensive, affordable, easy, quick, luxurious, clinical, medical, specialist, fresh, young, etc, these are all words that could be used to define your brands personality. What words would you like associated with your brands personality? Use these words when trying to name your business or create a slogan.

Keep a list of the words you choose and when creating any part of your business remind yourself and your team of the brands personality and image.

Relationship with the client

What does the brand say about the client who uses it? The black American Express card immediately tells us that the owner is very wealthy and a member of the exclusive few black Amex card holders. The "Mum's love Iceland" slogan from the Iceland adverts suggests to me that Iceland shoppers are budget conscious, down to earth, responsible adults who need quick and easy food solutions for the family. Nail Haven (my former chain of nail salon's based in Selfridges&Co) clients seemed to say that they were busy, high-end shoppers / city dwellers, who appreciated a fast, fuss free but high quality nail service.

The benefits of branding

Why bother creating a brand for your business? Well, for one, it would mean that you would have taken time to think through your entire salon offering, considering everything from its look, treatment list, prices, etc, to its customer service policies, therefore creating a coherent, well-presented package rather than a mishmash of too many ideas. Secondly, if your brand is successful in creating and maintaining a strong positive impression in the clients mind then you have also created a valuable asset as well as the opportunity to expand your business using this brand. Another benefit of branding is that it will help you differentiate yourself from your competitors, making your unique selling points more obvious to your clients, therefore making it easier for them to choose you!

◎ Creating a strong, appealing brand is one of the most important things you can do in marketing... your brand will be one of your most powerful attraction tools!

What are you offering your client and is this expressed in your brand?

Creating the right impression through branding
A successful brand is one which creates and maintains a strong positive impression in the clients mind. This impression is made up of the following main parts:-

* The business name and logo;
* Its presentation and packaging;
* Its reputation

Business Name and Logo

Choosing your company or trading name and logo is one of the main elements of creating a brand and therefore an important part of your marketing plan. Take your time with this and make sure the name reflects what you are trying to get across to your customer!

A good method of choosing a name would be to use a thesaurus to create a full list of all the words that are relevant to your offering or that describe a specific concept or feeling. Then spend some time combining them in different ways to come up with a name that is appealing to you and your target market. Remember to also search the thesaurus for the words you used to describe your brands personality earlier.

■ Example

Obviously words like 'beauty', 'health' and 'pamper' are relevant to this business. Looking at the thesaurus available in Microsoft Word, I get the following list of related words:-

Beauty	Health	Pamper	Location
Gorgeous	Fitness	Treat	Site
Exquisite	Wellbeing	Spoil	Position
Pretty	Strength	Indulge	Place
Lovely	Vigour	Protect	Spot
Good looks	Shape	Cherish	Scene
Attractive	Happiness	Treasure	Dwelling
Splendour	Comfort		Area
			Space
			Zone

So a few salon names from the above list could be:-

Gorgeous You
Indulge Me
The Splendid Nail Shop
Massage Zone
The Pretty Space
A Pretty Place
BEAUTY by professionals

...and so on. This process could take a few days; it may take a while to find the perfect word to describe your business but it is there, just keep looking and get your friends involved!

When you have made a list of possible business names, you will need to check whether they are available and not being used by other businesses. This can be done by going onto the Companies House web site (www.companieshouse.gov.uk) and checking company name availability and also by checking the Patent Office web site (www.ipo.gov.uk) and seeing if the name has been registered as a trade mark, i.e., ®

Once you have chosen your business name you should have a business logo created. A logo is a recognizable graphic design element, representing an organization or product. This logo will represent your business! Make sure it is the correct representation! Consider colours, styling and fonts carefully.

If you can afford to have a graphics designer create one for you then chose this option. A good designer will charge around £250 or £35/hour to design about 4 logos for you to choose from. They should provide you with the logo in at least the following formats; as an .eps, .jpg and .gif files. You will especially want the .eps file, as this format has no size limitations. You will then have the freedom to use your logo on business cards, price lists, posters, shop signage, business plans, the web site, etc. Agree on payment terms with the designer before work starts; what if you don't like the logos? Also make sure you have full and sole rights to your logo and anything else the designer creates for you.

I think using a graphics designer for this is a good investment and I highly recommend (UK) Swoop Media - www.swoopmedia.com

Swoop Media offer the full design solution, including printing jobs at very reasonable prices.

Remember to provide any company or individual you use with a proper brief on who you are targeting and what you have in mind.

A registered trade mark...
You should make your company name and logo a Registered Trade Mark, that way no one else can use it and if you become hugely successful it could be worth something.

In the UK, registering your trade mark yourself will cost you from £200. Visit www.patent.gov.uk for more on this.

The Presentation & Packaging Of Your Services & Product

Salon styling; furniture, atmosphere, uniforms, greeting, etc
The way your salon is designed and staff are dressed all contribute towards your businesses overall presentation. These should all work well with the salons name and logo design.

What look are you going to go for; sleek, friendly, bright, fresh, modern, classical, etc? Will the atmosphere be warm and luxurious or fresh and bright? Try to plan these things down to the last detail (including uniforms, towels, client welcome, everything) before execution and save yourself costly mistakes.

Treatment list and pricing
Your treatment list and the names of your treatments need to be relevant and appeal to your market. For example there is no point offering elaborate colourful nail art designs and investing in airbrush machines and staff training if your potential clients are French manicure lovers! Instead, I would focus my efforts on ensuring that any potential French manicure loving customers know that we give the best French manicures in town!

Also pricing your treatments incorrectly can be detrimental to your success. For example charging £5 for a blow dry when the going rate is £25 can firstly bankrupt you, and secondly make any potential clients wonder what's wrong with your hairdryers!

Some salons have made it part of their brand image to give their treatments funky names and follow this language through in other customer communications. For example, Bliss Spa use a very specific style when communicating with their clients and have been very successful in getting their target market to love their service and easily recognise their brand; see www.blissworld.com

Product list and the brands you use and retail
Your salons use and retail product list needs to be comprehensive

and offer your clients real results and home beauty maintenance. The brands you choose to stock also affect your own brand by association. Choose brands that are in line with your image, pricing and offer.

How your products are displayed is also a factor; see more on merchandising in *i* chapter 9, Retail, chapter 5, Making Money and chapter 10, Reception Area.

Salon literature and other stationery

As mentioned above, the language, tone and font you use to communicate with your customers in writing is part of your brand image. It needs to be consistent; in the same style throughout all your communications. You could decide to adopt a straight-forward & practical, funny & girly, elegant & stylish or whatever else comes to mind, approach to your written communications. Again, as always, keep the same themes going throughout all the branding exercise, and of course, always appealing to your market.

Reputation

Building the best reputation for your business builds the reputation of your brand and will be crucial to a successful value-adding branding exercise. Your salons reputation will mainly be based around the quality of the customer service and treatments offered. This all implies that your staff hiring and training programme directly affects your marketing plan. Please read *i* chapters 12 and 7 on Customer Service and Staff.

As mentioned in those chapters, word of mouth is king; if your clients are talking positively about your salon and recommending it, your salon-brand will slowly start to be valued and associated with quality, effectiveness or/and value for money.

---

5. Planning a Launch, Promotional and Advertising Campaigns

Launch day

Needless to say, your launch day is a very special day; full of nerves and excitement! You should plan something special for your first day of trading, whilst still being fully functional and able to give clients the best treatments... remember, they must want to come back!

Something to definitely consider pre-launch day is displaying a large sign on your shop window or hoarding around your intended location, telling passers-by what is opening and when.

Ideas for your launch day are discussed fully in *i* chapter 17, Launch day, however, in terms of marketing keep the style of the day in line with all your branding efforts.

Press and advertising

The best form of advertising is editorial, meaning instead of paying for a space in a magazine, local newspaper or billboard, you get an article written about you, your business or some other unique issue linked to your business. This is not only free but much more likely to get the attention of your market. These days consumers are bombarded with adverts and as such, small one-off ads seem to have little impact. Of course it is difficult to get editorial; you have to capture the attention of magazine and newspaper editors who are all also bombarded by other people wanting articles written about them. For this reason you will have to provide editors with great stories or unique perspectives on your situation. Usually businesses hire PR agencies to do this for them. A PR agency will use all its professional networks and expertise to get you or your product and service in every relevant publication. Most PR agencies cost a lot of money, however if this is in your marketing budget then go for it, but make sure the company you use is a good one with references and a track record of results!

If you can't afford a PR agency you can try doing it yourself. You will need to write your own articles and other press communications that are catchy and interesting, and then try and get them out through as many mediums as possible. A great, practical and easy to use book that can help you achieve PR success is 'Get Noticed' by Paula Gardner; it is available through a site called www.doyourownpr.com (Do your own PR) – great name, straight to the point I think!

Here are some ideas on how to get press interested in your salon:-

- Have a press day; invite members of the relevant press to your salon for a day of treatments and nibbles. Open the salon just for them, gear up your team to really impress the visitors and give them something to write about!

- Jump on the band wagon of an interesting current event or issue. For example, if the big story of the day is all about the effects of a poor diet on the skin, you could put together an article on this adding that certain body treatments can alleviate the discomfort, including your salon as one of the places offering this treatment...

- Put together a press pack including a one-pager on your salon with great pictures, your beautiful pricelist, some free samples, a gift voucher, etc. Really highlight your USP making it exciting news!

 Again, get your thinking cap on and try and imagine what would interest you if you had 10 different salons all trying to get you to write about them!

When you do manage to get a good article written about you then think about displaying it in the salon and salon window.

As for paying for adverts, choose the medium wisely for maximum effect. Also, if you've managed to build a brand with a good reputation you may like to get short quotes and testimonials from

your clients and use them on leaflets or adverts.

Building and using a client database
In *i* chapter 11, On-Going Management I covered maintaining client records in detail, how you use their details is mainly a marketing function.

In the UK you will need to know and respect the Data Protection Act 1998. It provides a framework to ensure that personal information is handled properly.

It states that anyone who processes personal information must comply with eight principles, to make sure that personal information is:-

- Fairly and lawfully processed; only hold information that you obtained through the correct channels
- Processed for limited purposes; clients must know what you plan to do with their information
- Adequate, relevant and not excessive; don't ask for more or less information than you actually need
- Accurate and up to date
- Not kept for longer than is necessary
- Processed in line with the individuals rights; their right being that they are allowed access to any information held about them
- Secure; make sure the information is not accessed by unauthorised persons
- Not transferred to other countries without adequate protection

Find more information on the Data Protection Act on the Information Commissioners Office web site; www.ico.gov.uk

Keeping this in mind, decide how you plan to use this data. You may decide that you will create a quarterly newsletter; maybe your salon introduces new products or new treatments regularly and you would like to let your clients know about this. You may also have sales, seasonal promotions or run special customer evenings and events that you could advertise to your clients. Try and keep you communications relevant and in the style of your business. Don't bombard your clients with too many letters; they will just stop reading them or even worse, get irritated!

Sales, promotions, offers, special events
Remember the purpose of promotions are to get new clients through your door or/and existing clients coming back to you. However, it is quite a well known fact in business that it is less costly to keep existing clients than to find new ones. Try and keep your existing clients coming back to you through great customer service and loyalty rewards (see next section and chapter 12) and focus your promotions on getting new clients through the door. This does not mean that your existing clients should not benefit from any promotions; I just mean keep your promotions budget for new business and consider it successful when you can add more satisfied clients to your list.

Please note that this is just a suggestion and the best way to offer promotions all depends on your particular salon. For instance you may have hundreds of one-visit clients on your records. This situation needs you to contact them with some sort of incentive to return. Another scenario may be that your business benefits from more than average passing trade and as such you have many new clients everyday but maybe due to location not so many regulars. This scenario would require that you give those people who go out of their way to come back to you, extra thanks for their loyalty; this may be in the form of special discounts.

Promotion and special event suggestions:-

• Seasonal promotions (winter, spring, summer and autumn) and celebration promos (mother's day, valentines day, etc) are the most obvious but don't only need to consist of discounts on treatments and products, they can also include limited edition items, available only during that period.
• Open days or open weeks! Advertise an open day at the salon, especially in your shop window welcoming everyone to come in and ask questions, discuss their beauty needs or sample

products and treatments.
* Client evenings
* Birthday discounts

Be creative, be different, think about what you would like to get, ask others what they would like to get or what has enticed them in the past but always remember to manage the costs and see that the exercise is a profitable one.

Loyalty points & other rewards

Regular clients should be appreciated and rewarded for their loyalty. A loyalty point system would generally consist of clients collecting points with every visit and then after collecting a set amount, redeem them against treatments. You could also see that very loyal clients are not subject to salon price increases. Or once a certain spend limit is reached in a year, you could give the client a little goody-bag of their favourite products or new products to try. Again be creative but never forget your profit margins!

Web site

A web site is an amazing and essential marketing tool. Apart from the obvious fact that you can sell all the products you have in your salon online with minimal extra effort; your web site is also another major advertising avenue for the salon. Information about your treatments, prices, location and team are essential for those searching the local area on the internet or looking for specific beauty treatments or products that you provide. The other great thing about having a web site is that after the initial cost of having the site designed and built, the on-going maintenance costs are relatively inexpensive. A definite worthwhile investment!

Have an effective, professional and beautifully created web site designed and built for you through Miss Salon™ from just £420. Visit www.misssalon.com for more information and contact details.

6. Contingency Plans...

If your advertising and promotional efforts don't work then you will need plan B. Don't allow disappointment to get you down. Get your thinking cap on and start again! This may be a good time to have a mystery shopper and do a full salon inspection to try and figure out what's been going wrong. Are previous clients coming back? If not, then why not? Are your clients recommending your salon to their friends? If not, then why not? Are potential clients able to find you, access your service easily, is your service any good, overpriced or relevant? It maybe that your salon is great but your advertising efforts haven't been effective and you need to try something different.

Be objective and have a Plan B

SETTING MARKETING TARGETS

I explain how to set sales targets in *i* chapter 14, Finances and Accounting. However, marketing targets, whilst ultimately need to convert into cash, may be more about seeing an increase in client numbers or reaching a wider audience.

For example, say your salon has struggled with increasing footfall through the door and as such revenue was stagnant or worse in decline. To address this lack of new business, your marketing plan for the following year or quarter could include:-

• Having a web site built;
• Organising 4 client evenings and 1 open-week in the summer.

You would measure the success of these exercises by the number of new clients you managed to gain and then ultimately by the increase in revenue (assuming you don't lose any of your regulars) for that period. So one of your marketing targets in this plan would be to increase client numbers by a certain percentage.

Further reading and information
There are many books out there on marketing. Marketing can be quite a complicated subject and many of these books can get too detailed, however if you need more information or assistance in this area the following books have been quite useful to me:-

* **The Little Book With Big Impact For Day Spas - John Uhrig *****
* Marketing for Dummies – Alexander Hiam
* Marketing Communications – Chris Fill

All of the above can be purchased at www.misssalon.com

Web sites with more information...
www.about.com
www.wikipedia.org/wiki/Marketing
www.smallbusiness.co.uk

Chapter Summary

Most entrepreneurs starting out have a vision of how they want their salon to look and function; this is fantastic as it is the start of your dream becoming a reality. However, this vision needs to be formalised into a marketing plan, ensuring that the businesses position, presentation and operations are aligned for maximum sales and long term success. Never stop marketing!

A final comment...
Please understand one thing... the lovely furniture, wonderful logo, great products and super offers won't mean a thing if the actual treatments are ineffective or performed badly; your team must be the best you can get and on-point with their skills! This is an absolute must.

Chapter 14
FINANCE & ACCOUNTING

Does it all add up?

Money, money, money!

CAPITAL EXPENDITURE

How Much Do You Need To Start Your Business?

Capital Expenditure is simply the money you spend starting your business. It is every penny you spend setting up your salon before you actually start trading.

Below is a typical list of the costs you can expect to incur starting your salon: -

(Please note that there may be other costs that are specific to your situation; these may not appear on the list, but need to be added)

- Shop deposit
- 3 months Rent
- 3 months Business Rates
- Premium, if any
- Shop-fit, including furniture, fixtures, fittings and decorating
- Solicitors Fees
- Stock
- Equipment
- Licensing
- Insurance
- Telephone line(s)
- Computer and printer
- Broadband
- Salon and business stationery; including price lists, business cards, etc
- Company registration fees, if applicable
- Web site

Capital expenditure is also known as capital costs, capital investment or investment costs. The money that you spend to start your business is seen as an investment. It is an investment because this money has been spent with the idea of making more money. It is expected to grow through either the service of the business or the assets owned by the business.

What Does It Cost To Set Up A Salon?

This is up to you; your vision and your budget. On average, in the UK, I would say that you would need an absolute minimum of £10,000 to £15,000 to start a very small salon, maybe within another operation, i.e., a shopping centre or a shop.

■ For example
My very first nail bar located in Topshop Oxford Circus, London, consisted of:-

- 1 custom-made table (with built-in storage and air-filters)
- 6 custom-made client chairs
- 6 technician's chairs
- 1 airbrush machine
- Stock for 6 stations plus
- 1 lit 'Nail Haven' sign
- A home office, including computer, printer, fax/copier, desks, chairs, etc.

The above, including all other capital expenditure listed on the previous page, cost me around £25,000 to start. That was without shop deposits, rent, rates or web site, as being in Topshop cancelled that requirement. Quite expensive, huh! However, as time went on and I opened more salons, I found more affordable ways of having furniture made and creating even better salons! The point being that if you plan properly and search hard enough you can make your budget stretch further and still have reasonable quality. The above is really only to give you an idea of where to start; the capital costs will totally depend on the types of treatments offered, location, style, size and so on of your business.

Contingency Money

This is some extra money, maybe in savings, as an overdraft or agreed from an investor in case your business has a slow start. It is not really Capital as you may or may not use it. This is usually around 3 to 6 months worth of business costs, allowing your salon this time to get going. I know it is already tough to try and raise enough Capital without having to add extra thousands in case of bad days, but trust me, in the beginning there will be bad days and getting through those whilst being creative is much easier when you can still pay your bills.

Your P&L and Cash flow forecasts will help you plan for and estimate what contingency money you need to raise.

RAISING FINANCE

I know this is the biggest question on most entrepreneurs' minds.

Where do I get the money from to start my business??

The first thing I would say here is that if you are serious about starting your business, if you are passionate and can think of nothing else other than getting your salon open; you will raise the money you need to do it... because where there's a will, there's a way!

Second, open your mind to all the potential ways in which you could raise capital. Remember that if you have a business plan; properly researched and well presented, you are half way there. Any potential investor or lender will see you as a serious person to entrust with their money. Not a dreamer, a talker or someone who hasn't thought things through properly, but a business person aiming to grow their money, their investment!

Think about when you may have needed to borrow money from someone in your life. You may have needed a small (or large) amount for a few days while you wait for funds to come to you from another avenue. What do you say, "lend me some money till, Friday when I get paid"? You automatically give the person an idea of when they are going to get their money back and how come you will have it at that time. You may even tell them why you need it.
Well, seeking funding for your business is no different. You will have to explain what you will use the money for, but much more importantly when you will return it and through what means.

Without a business plan you will struggle to convince anyone to part with any amount of money. When will they get it back? How much are they going to get back? Are they better off putting their cash into a savings account; what are the returns on investment? How are you going to pay it back? How do you know that it is going to work?

The other thing to recognise when seeking funding is the fact that investors and lenders are investing in YOU! You have to instil enthusiasm and confidence into your audience! If you don't know the answers to the all-important financial questions, or you seem confused or arrogant or worse, uninspired (!), then they are less likely to want to put their money in your charge. Raising finance can take a while. Expect this process to take anything from 6 months to a year; with business plan changes, updates and equity negotiations, what may initially have seemed straightforward to you, may not be the case for the people you approach. So don't be disheartened, it all works towards improving your plan and forecasts, your understanding of your business and therefore its eventual success!

The Difference Between A Loan and An Investment

Whether or not the business succeeds, a loan will need to be paid

back, either in instalments or in one lump sum with a set interest rate. An investment does not need to be paid back if the business is unsuccessful.

Big difference!

When meeting with your potential investor, make sure you look good, act the part and know your stuff!

Here is a list of likely money-raising avenues:-

- Family and friends
- Business Link, The Princes Trust and other business support organisations
- The Bank
- Partnerships
- Business Angels
- Venture Capitalists
- Your savings and assets

Get your "open-mind" thinking cap on and don't stop brainstorming money raising ideas until you have a list of at least 10 action steps.

Friends and Family

Friends and family should be your first port of call. They know you best, know your dreams and know what you are capable of. If they have any access to money, being able to convince them of your potential and the potential of your venture should be achievable with a good plan. Even if they don't have any money to invest, ask them to read your plan and tell you what they think of it; would they invest if they could? Why would they invest or not? This all helps towards perfecting the plan and therefore the impression you are giving potential investors.

A small word of caution; even though it may be your dad, mum or best-friends boyfriend offering you the money, please try to keep this part of your relationship as professional as possible. Be clear as to whether the money is an investment or a loan. Have any special terms of the exchange written down.

Business Link, The Princes Trust and other business support organisations

In the UK there are many government and private organisations that offer loans or grants to help set up small businesses. These organisations will have different criteria for acceptance, ranging from you being within a certain age bracket, to your business being in a particular industry. Search the internet for these organisations. Business Link is one of the most useful organisations in this respect; both for offering grants and loans and also for providing up-to-date information. Please visit www.businesslink. gov.uk Also visit:- www.j4b.co.uk - A comprehensive guide to grant information for the UK & Ireland. Find Grants, Loans, Tax Relief, Venture Capital and Awards to support your organisation. And the Princes Trust web site www.princes-trust.org.uk. For outside the UK, search for similar organisations online.

The Bank

Yes, the bank *(sigh)*... well, firstly understand that the banks are not interested in investing in your business; all they are interested in is the risks associated with lending you (that is, you) money. Your credit rating, your assets, your banking history, whether or not you have a guarantor backing you, your own personal financial investment and the success rating of the industry your business is part of, are really the only factors that will affect whether or not they lend you (that is, you) money! Your level of experience in the business or your businesses profit & loss forecast are all secondary factors; these things are important in terms of the overall impression you give but not in terms of whether their loan will be repaid!

i See chapter... ◎ Get it done ⚲ Thinking time ■ Example ☺ You can do it!

Please note that if your business has already been trading for a few years and you have good financial records for those years, showing a profitable business with positive cash flow, then a bank may consider lending to you based on that... although ironically, that's probably when you least need the money!

Basically, in general, a bank's decision will be based on hard cold numbers and credit scores, and not on feelings, gut instinct or whether you have the best business idea in the whole wide world! So don't be disappointed or put off if they don't give you cash when you first approach them, however, you should approach them nevertheless. In terms of your financial forecasts, Banks are most interested in your cash flow forecast. See Cash Flow later in this chapter.

Partnerships
As mentioned in *i* chapter 4, Business Structure, for many reasons you may want to start your business with another person. This could be to share the capital costs of the venture or to pull all your assets and other resources together to have a better chance of getting a bank loan and such. As with friends and family ensure that all the terms of your partnership are written down and signed by all parties!

Business Angels (BA)
Business Angels are people who invest in companies that have good growth potential. They are like the successful, investing, entrepreneurs on the television programme, Dragons Den. Business Angels invest anything from £10,000 - £750,000. They are usually quite knowledgeable and experienced in business and for that reason can make decisions quite quickly about whether or not they want to invest in your venture. They are also able to add their expertise to your business, thus further increasing your chances of success.

Sounds great; well beware; they can be very shrewd and are only interested in the returns on investment (ROI). So have your wits about you and only settle for what you are happy with.
In terms of your financial forecasts, BA's are most interested in your

profit and loss forecasts, because they are investing in the future profits of your business. See P&L later in this chapter. Of course they also want to know that you understand the importance of cash flow and have planned well for the future, thereby minimising the need to come back asking for more money a few months down the line!

Venture Capitalists (VC)

Venture Capital is also known as Private Equity Finance. Unlike business angels, venture capitalists look to invest large sums of money in return for some of your business' shares. If you plan to open one or two salons VCs are not for you. They typically focus on much bigger propositions. For instance if you already own 5 to 10 salons or have a large client database through online sales or a catalogue and you want to expand further, maybe launching a private label, then there will be VCs interested in investing.

More information
British Business Angels Association www.bbaa.gov.uk.
British Venture Capital Association www.bvca.co.uk.
Also visit Business Link www.businesslink.gov.uk

For outside the UK, search for similar organisations online.

Savings and Assets

Another way of raising capital for your business is to save money over a period of time. Generally speaking this is usually not that feasible if you are only able to put away a small amount each month. However, if your current employment pays out bonuses, you receive a redundancy package or some other lump sum, then you may be able to put a substantial amount aside for your business. If you do already have savings, then great, go ahead and invest your money in your wonderful business... after all, why should anyone else do so if you won't, right? However, just as an **extra tip**, try all your other options first before using all your own money, especially if you have dependants. Limit your risk, even if you have come up with the best business idea in the whole wide world!

 i See chapter... ◎ Get it done ♀ Thinking time ■ Example ☺ You can do it!

Other Sources Of Information On Raising Finance

Visit www.bbaa.gov.uk
Click the link to the article, Finance Your High Growth Business –
Paul Gardner

Also www.j4b.co.uk
A comprehensive guide to grant information for the UK & Ireland.
Find Grants, Loans, Tax Relief, Venture Capital and Awards to support
your organisation.

FINANCIAL FORECASTS

Predicting how much money your business will generate and how
much it will cost to generate it, is probably the most important aspect
of any business; doing this will immediately highlight whether or not
your business idea is viable and worth pursuing.

Basically, a great idea is not a great idea until you do the numbers!

Your financial forecasts will consist of the following:-

- Cash Flow (at least 3 years)
- Profit & Loss (at least 3 years)
- Assumptions and Calculations**
- Balance Sheet
- Breakeven Calculation
- Return On Investment

To produce these forecasts, you will need to work out the
following:-

- Direct Costs
- Indirect Costs
- Revenue
- Assets
- Share distribution / Ownership

** When estimating costs, revenue and assets you will need to make a few assumptions and do some calculations based on those assumptions. These assumptions and calculations must be presented in the business plan so that it is clear how you made your predictions and therefore created your profit forecasts.

We will look at costs, revenue and assets first and then go on to the forecasts.

Direct Costs

Direct costs are the expenses that are incurred *only* when a product is sold or a treatment is given. For example, to give a client a haircut you have to have the undivided use of a space in the salon, some shampoo and the hairdresser - These are therefore direct costs. The cost of water and electricity used cannot be pinpointed to one client and are therefore indirect costs. The scissors, hair dryer, chair and till used are part of the initial capital expenditure and are assets of the business. Hence the following are your standard salons direct costs:-

- Rent
- Salaries
- Stock
- License**

**Depending on your location, you may not be allowed to trade without a license so it makes the direct costs list.

Indirect Costs (Overheads)

Indirect costs are all the other expenses incurred when running a business. These costs are also known as overheads. Because overheads are not associated directly with providing the service as direct costs are, if your business runs into financial difficulty, you will often be advised to try and reduce your overheads as your first action.

The following are typical indirect costs / overheads:-

* MD/Owner salary
* Professional services
* Web site maintenance
* Loan repayments
* Bank fees
* Telephone Bills / Broadband
* Utilities
* Insurance
* Printing and Stationery
* Depreciation**
* Miscellaneous (staff outings, travel, etc)

**Depreciation is a way of calculating how long your salons assets and equipment will last. For example, the hair dryer or airbrush machine will not last forever. If you expect your £30 hair dryer to last at least 3 years after which time you have to buy another one, then each year its value will deprecate by £10. The same goes for the work stations, chairs, reception desk, the salons fixtures and fittings. How long will they last and at what cost will they need to be renewed?

Revenue / Turnover / Income / Sales

The businesses revenue forecast requires you to clearly understand and calculate how much money you think your business will generate, every day, week, month and year.

There are various ways of doing this, but all your calculations will depend on the number of money–making stations in your salon, your prices, treatment duration times and on the research you have done into the location of your salon; your target market and their shopping habits.

It is very important to be as realistic as possible when forecasting and to be modest with your expectations; that way you will be better prepared if business doesn't boom straightaway.

Treatment Sales Calculations
To start, calculate your revenue when working at maximum capacity, meaning all your operators busy, all your stations busy.

■ For example
A beauty salon has 6 money making stations (MMS) offering a range of treatments; nails, hair, facials.
1 nail station
3 hair stations
2 facial stations

There are 8 trading hours in a day and the salon is open 6 days a week.

In 8 hours the nail station can do:-
6 mini manicures 20 minutes each, £10 each (total 120 minutes, £60)
4 full sets of acrylic nails 90 minutes each, £50 (total 360 minutes, £200) Total time = 480 minutes = 8 hours

**Total nail station revenue = £260 in one very busy day
(Please also note the number of clients = 10)**

In 8 hours the hair station can do:-
6 cut and blow-dry, 45 minutes each, £35 each (total 270 minutes, £210)
2 colour and cut, 90 minutes each, £75 each (total 180 minutes, £150)

---

i See chapter... ◎ Get it done ♔ Thinking time ■ Example ☺ You can do it!

Total time = 450 minutes = 7.5 hours

Total hair station revenue = £360 in one very busy day
3 hair stations = £360 x 3 = £1,080 per day
(Please also note the number of clients = 8 x 3 stations = 24)

In 8 hours, the facial stations can do:-
8 facials, 60 minutes each, £40 each (total 480 minutes, £320)
Total time = 480 minutes = 8 hours

Total facial station revenue = £320 in one very busy day
2 facial stations = £320 x 2 = £640 per day
(Please also note the number of clients = 8 x 2 stations = 16)

Therefore, in one day, working at maximum capacity (100%), the salon can generate the following:-

Revenue = £260 + £1080 + £640 =	**£1,980**
Clients = 10 + 24 + 16 =	**50**
Client average spend = £1980 ÷ 50 =	**£39.60**

Therefore, the revenue forecasts for 5 different capacity levels would be:-

Treatment Revenue	at 100%	at 75%	at 50%	at 25%	at 10%
Daily client numbers	50	37.5	25	12.5	5
Daily	£1,980	£1,485	£990	£495	£198
Weekly (£1980 x 6 days)	£11,880	£8,910	£5,940	£2,970	£1,188
Monthly ((£11,880 x 51 weeks) ÷ 12)	£50,490	£37,868	£25,245	£12,623	£5,049
Yearly (£11,880 x 51 weeks)	£605,880	£454,410	£302,940	£151,470	£60,588

51 weeks in the year due to salon closures for Christmas, New Years day, etc

Next, based on the location and the target market, you can try to estimate whether you could get 50 customers through your door in one day or if it's more likely that you would get 5 per day. You could think about the time of year; maybe December will be at 75% while June at 25% and January at 10%.

Working out the revenues at different capacities in this way will allow you to attempt to be more accurate in your yearly forecasts.

Also remember that these calculations are based only on treatment sales and not product retail. Another point, notice in your estimates which service brings in the most revenue. In this example the hair stations generate the most income per station. This information can help you decide how much space to allocate to each type of service in your salon. Here I have given hair the most salon space with 3 stations.

Product Sales Calculations
One way to forecast this figure is to estimate for instance that 2 in every 10 clients to the salon buy products. That is 20% of customers buy.

So based on the previous client numbers, you could forecast the following:-

Product Sales	at 100%	at 75%	at 50%	at 25%	at 10%
Daily client numbers	50	37.5	25	12.5	5
Daily products sold	10	8	5	3	1
Weekly products sold (x 6 days)	60	45	30	15	6
Monthly products sold (x 51 wks ÷ 12)	255	191	128	64	26
Yearly products sold (x 51 wks)	3060	2295	1530	765	306

Calculated as follows = if 20% of clients buy, then from 50 clients, 10 would buy (50 x 20%)

If the average product sale is £7 (you will need to work out what an average product costs in your salon), then you can go on to calculate the revenue based on that.

Product Revenue	at 100%	at 75%	at 50%	at 25%	at 10%
Average product price	£7.00	£7.00	£7.00	£7.00	£7.00
Daily products sold	£70.00	£52.50	£35.00	£17.50	£7.00
Weekly products sold (x 6 days)	£420.00	£315.00	£210.00	£105.00	£42.00
Monthly products sold (x 51 wks ÷ 12)	£1,785.00	£1,338.75	£892.50	£446.25	£178.50
Yearly products sold (x 51 wks)	£21,420.00	£16,065.00	£10,710.00	£5,355.00	£2,142.00

Use this example to help you calculate and forecast your revenue.

If you have difficulty with this you can purchase the calculation templates from Miss Salon™ at www.misssalonbusiness.com

Assets

An asset is either cash or anything that can be turned into cash. Tangible assets include land, buildings, fixtures and fittings, stock, machinery, cash and so on. Intangible assets include goodwill, copyrights, patents and trademarks. Assets can also be described as being fixed or current. Examples of tangible fixed assets are land and buildings, fixtures and fittings, equipment. Current, short term or circulating assets are assets that are constantly changing form, circulating from cash to goods to cash again. Examples are stock, cash and debtors.

Assets can appreciate or depreciate over time. In this business, the salon fixtures and fittings are likely to depreciate quite significantly in a short space of time. For example, you would struggle to sell any of the salons furniture for even half of their original price. Cash could appreciate in a savings account. Salon stock would depreciate but only slightly. With great customer service, the goodwill could appreciate hugely. And if the salon was in bought premises, and there is a boom in property prices, the buildings worth should appreciate.

Being able to forecast the value of your businesses assets is required for the P&L and for your Balance Sheet.

Ideally you would want your businesses assets to total a greater value than its total short-term and long-term debts. This would mean a positive balance sheet and you would be in a comfortable position should anything go wrong with the business or your circumstances change and you need to move on quickly.

When or if you want to sell your salon, its balance sheet, and therefore asset worth, will be vital in the valuation. See heading on balance sheets later in this chapter.

Share Distribution Or Dividing The Business

Shares are only relevant when dealing with a company; i.e., a business registered with Companies House as a limited company. A sole trader or business partnership registered for tax does not have shares and so dividing the profits or costs of this partnership is done based on the initial written or verbal agreements made between the partners.

What is a share?
Shares are equal parts of the capital stock of a company. When you register a limited company you will need to decide how many shares your company will have. Shares grant their owner a legal right to the part of the company's profits and to any voting rights attached to those shares.

When starting out it is probably best to register 100% of the company with 100 shares at £1 per share. That way it will be quite straight forward for you, when raising capital, to decide how much of the company's shares you want to allocate to the investor. If in future you need to increase the number of shares in the company, this is easily done by an accountant.

Introducing new shareholders
If for example you initially set up the company with 100 shares, as described above, and allocate 80 to you and 20 to another person. When or if you want to introduce another shareholder to the business you could give them some of your shares only and not affect the person who owns the 20, or you could dilute both ownerships. This is best handled by an accountant as this can affect the valuation of your business and have tax implications.

In any case when offering a stake of your company to an investor, it is always best to speak in terms of percentages rather than in number of shares. Just remember that a registered company is a legal entity and as a director you work for it and should only do what's best for the company and its shareholders! So until you get a good grip on this, it is always best to speak with your accountant on any company matters relating to share distribution, financing, selling, profit sharing, personal gains, personal expenses, etc.

Dividing the business – A Partnership
If your business is not a registered company then you are free to decide how you want to distribute ownership and profit share with no legal consequences outside of your partnership agreement.

Now that the costs, revenue, assets and shares have been understood, we can go on to understand and workout the forecasts...

Cash Flow

Cash flow is the movement of cash into and out of a business. Cash flow management is the regular monitoring of the businesses money, crucially including pre-empting and planning for future cash requirements. For your business plan you will need to show the cash flow forecast for between 3 to 5 years.

What is the difference between cash flow and profit & loss? Why is cash flow so important to a business?

■ I will use an example to explain cash flow verses profit. Say you earned £400 a week and your outgoings were £350 per week. This leaves you with £50 positive cash flow for other expenses.

Say it unexpectedly became freezing cold and you needed to buy a coat. The coat you need costs £150. Based on your income and outgoings it would take 3 weeks before you could buy this coat. But you need the coat now; you can't wait 3 weeks.

In this scenario if we looked at a one month (4 weeks) profit and loss of your account we would see that you would have earned £1,600, spent £1,400 and then a further £150 on a coat leaving you with a profit of £50 at the end of the month.

However, if we look at your cash flow for that same month we will see that for 3 weeks you were unable to pay for a crucial item. You had negative cash flow.

Say that coat was so crucial that without it you couldn't go to work and therefore risked losing your income of £400 altogether! This situation shows that a lack of cash, negative cash flow, was ultimately going to ruin you.

So you can have a situation whereby you could eventually be profitable but potentially suffer major business setbacks due to a lack of cash.

Unfortunately, borrowing money to solve this problem could affect your profits. For instance, if you had to repay the loan of £100 at the end of the month at say 30% interest (some awful credit card), this equates to a total payout of £130. So instead of a profit of £50, you are now left with £20... all because you didn't have the cash you needed when you needed it!

For this reason, temporary cash flow issues are best solved by doing one or more of the following:-

- Negotiating temporary extended payment terms with your suppliers or creditors, therefore freeing up some cash;

- Arranging an overdraft facility on your business account, rather than a loan; this can provide a temporary cash solution;

i See chapter... ◎ Get it done ᕯ Thinking time ■ Example ☺ You can do it!

- Selling some salon assets, like excess stock.

The above example is a very simplified version of what happens in business. Usually it is on a much larger scale and with stressful consequences, affecting many people.

Cash is king and staying in control of your cash flow is absolutely vital for the success of your business.

So what does staying in control of your cash flow mean and entail? Staying in control means:-

- To have a good idea of what the business can afford at any given time, i.e., budgeting
- Being able to pre-empt and plan for future cash requirements
- Not accidentally incur bank charges, fines or any other late payment penalties due to negligence or poor cash management!

A useful method of monitoring and managing your cash flow is by using a Microsoft Excel spreadsheet, loaded with all your businesses weekly income and outgoings. This document needs to be kept up to date with the latest cash situation and also look well into the future. When your business starts to thrive and has settled into a spending pattern, with a cash surplus then you may not have to be so meticulous with this spreadsheet. However, before that glorious time, I strongly recommend that you keep your spreadsheet updated at least once a week and make sure to always add any future expenses that you see coming, no matter how far away!

Don't ignore your cash flow forecast and what it's telling you! If you can't afford it, you can't afford it... yet!

You can buy a ready-made Miss Salon Cash Flow spreadsheet template (created in Microsoft Excel) for £15.99 from www. misssalonbusiness.com. It is easy to use and will amaze you at how well it will allow you to plan your cash future! This spreadsheet is also excellent for creating your first cash flow forecast, which you can print off to add to your business plan, as well as save on your computer for weekly updates.

Creating Your Own Cash Flow Spreadsheet

Looking at the example on the next page and using a Microsoft Excel workbook; create a cash flow spreadsheet by listing in the first column, all the sources or types of income your business generates and all the recipients your business pays. Then, decide in what intervals you want to see your cash flow; weekly or monthly (row 1). I suggest weekly to start. For example, if you do all your final banking on Fridays then make each of the following cash columns start on a Friday. What I mean is, label the top columns with the correct Friday date for at least one year (52 columns) (the example shows only the first 8 weeks; row 1 and columns 3-10). Once you have done this your basic template has been created.

Now you need to input the cash-in and the cash-out of the business within the correct week or month column, and in the corresponding income (rows 2-6) or recipient rows (rows 10-55). Total the incomes (A - row 8) and total the outgoings (B - row 57) for the week to find your net cash balance at the end of the week (row 59). This final balance should then be taken over to the next column and added to the following week's income (row 2). Notice that all incomes in row 2 are from the previous periods row 59.

If you have a basic knowledge of Excel, then you should be able to use formulas to do the calculations for you. If not, I suggest purchasing our ready-made spreadsheet template. It has all the formulas pre-

---

loaded, all you have to do is input the relevant recipient names and your actual figures or estimates.

Example of a businesses cash flow forecast:-

#	ACCOUNT NAME / ACCOUNT DETAILS	06-Aug-04	13-Aug-04	20-Aug-04	27-Aug-04	03-Sep-04	10-Sep-04	17-Sep-04	24-Sep-04	01-Oct-04
2	ACTUAL BANK BALANCE	£1,000.00	£412.00	£2,140.00	£3,074.50	£90.73	£16.73	£379.73	£40.73	£2,318.73
3	TREATMENTS SALES	£2,000.00	£1,567.00	£2,134.00	£2,200.00	£1,789.00	£1,899.00	£2,067.00	£2,089.00	£1,987.00
4	RETAIL SALES	£500.00	£300.00	£456.00	£134.00	£435.00	£564.00	£304.00	£256.00	£432.00
5	INTEREST	£0.00	£0.00	£0.00	£0.00	£0.00	£0.00	£0.00	£0.00	£0.00
6	OTHER INCOME	£0.00	£0.00	£0.00	£0.00	£0.00	£0.00	£0.00	£0.00	£0.00
7										
8	TOTAL INCOME (CASH-IN) A	£3,500.00	£2,279.00	£4,730.00	£5,408.50	£2,314.73	£2,479.73	£2,750.73	£2,385.73	£4,737.73
9										
10	MAIN SALARIES	£1,225.00		£1,655.50		£1,455.00		£1,677.00		£1,658.21
11	AGENCY STAFF									
12	PRIZE MONEY									
13	TRAINING									
14	REFUNDS	£23.00								
16	SUPPLIER 1	£235.00						£235.00		
17	SUPPLIER 2	£125.00						£125.00		
18	SUPPLIER 3	£754.00						£510.00		
19	SUPPLIER 4			£23.00						
20	SUPPLIER 5			£46.00						
21	SUPPLIER 6	£65.00						£65.00		
22	SUPPLIER 7	£98.00						£98.00		
23	SUPPLIER 8					£1,200.00		£2,100.00		
24	SUPPLIER 9					£869.00				
25	SUPPLIER 10									
26	SUPPLIER 11			£70.00						
27	SUPPLIER 12									
28	OTHER SUPPLIERS									
30	BANK INTEREST									
31	BANK CHARGES									
32	VAT					£1,383.77				
33	PAYE					£1,678.00				
34	TAX						£400.00			
35	LICENCE									
36	INSURANCE	£53.00						£53.00		£53.00
37	ACCOUNTANTS									
38	SOLICITORS									
39	LOAN REPAYMENTS	£360.00						£360.00		£360.00
40	PAYROLL COMPANY	£30.00						£30.00		£30.00
42	PARKING									
43	TRAVEL									
44	FINES									
45	FOOD									
46	HOTELS									
48	PRINTERS					£110.00				
49	STATIONERY / POST					£23.00				
50	PROMOTIONS / PR MATERIAL									
52	MOBILE PHONE					£54.00			£67.00	
53	LANDLINE PHONE	£120.00								
55	MISCELLANEOUS									
56										
57	TOTAL PAYMENTS (CASH-OUT) B	£3,088.00	£139.00	£1,655.50	£5,317.77	£2,298.00	£2,100.00	£2,710.00	£67.00	£2,101.21
58										
59	ACTUAL BANK BALANCE (A - B)		£412.00	£2,140.00	£3,074.50	£90.73	£16.73	£379.73	£40.73	£2,318.73	£2,636.53

Profit & Loss

Profit or loss is the money left after all costs have been paid. When preparing your business plan you will need to show P&L forecasts for between 3 to 5 years.

The P&L forecast is basically a way of displaying your predictions of the businesses sales less direct and indirect costs (see page 233). I will take you through a complete example in the next few pages.

There are three levels of profit or loss, these are:-

Gross Profit or Loss
This is the money left after paying direct costs only.

Net Profit or Loss
This is the money left after paying direct and indirect costs.

Net Profit or Loss After Taxation
This is the final money left after paying direct and indirect costs as well as corporation tax. This only affects registered companies, not sole traders. Sole traders will need to declare the businesses net profits and then pay individual personal tax on their share of those profits.

Another calculation that is also important for your P&L is the Gross Profit Percentage (GPP) (also known as *Gross Profit Margin* or *Gross Margin Ratio*). This is a strong indicator for financial performance and is calculated by dividing the gross profit by sales, times 100.

For example
Say the sales for month 1 was £15,000 and the direct costs were £10,000, then the gross profit for that month would be £15,000-£10,000 = £5,000.

Therefore, the Gross Profit Percentage (GPP) would be:-
(£5,000 ÷ £15,000) x 100 = **33.33%**

So why is the GPP such a strong indicator for financial performance?

This is because the GPP can only be improved if your sales go up and/or the direct costs come down!

◼ **Another example**
In this example, I reduce costs by £1000.

Sales = £15,000
Direct Costs = £9,000
Therefore, Gross Profit = £6,000
Therefore, GPP = **40%**

So in this second example it is clearer to an investor or owner that the business is being run more efficiently than in the first example; regardless of whether you can see the actual Sales or Direct Cost figures.

A respectable GPP for a business is around 30%. An experienced investor would not expect the GPP to fluctuate more than 3% to 4% unless you managed to make a very significant change to the businesses operations.

What could that sort of thing be??
Think! Is there a way that you could increase your sales without increasing your cost of sales?? Interesting...

Creating Your Own Profit & Loss Forecast

This may start to seem a little complex but stay focused and follow me in stages. Remember, we are trying to get the most realistic figures to complete the '?' in the table on the next page.

Firstly, for your P&L you will need your revenue/sales estimates. I will use the estimates calculated from the salon example on pages 235 to 237; these are displayed below again:-

Treatment Revenue	at 100%	at 75%	at 50%	at 25%	at 10%
Daily client numbers	50	37.5	25	12.5	5
Daily	£1,980	£1,485	£990	£495	£198
Weekly (£1980 x 6 days)	£11,880	£8,910	£5,940	£2,970	£1,188
Monthly ((£11,880 x 51 weeks) ÷ 12)	£50,490	£37,868	£25,245	£12,623	£5,049
Yearly (£11,880 x 51 weeks)	£605,880	£454,410	£302,940	£151,470	£60,588

51 weeks in the year due to salon closures for Christmas, New Years day, etc

Product Revenue	at 100%	at 75%	at 50%	at 25%	at 10%
Average product price	£7.00	£7.00	£7.00	£7.00	£7.00
Daily products sold	£70.00	£52.50	£35.00	£17.50	£7.00
Weekly products sold (x 6 days)	£420.00	£315.00	£210.00	£105.00	£42.00
Monthly products sold (x 51 wks ÷ 12)	£1,785.00	£1,338.75	£892.50	£446.25	£178.50
Yearly products sold (x 51 wks)	£21,420.00	£16,065.00	£10,710.00	£5,355.00	£2,142.00

Please note that, VAT must be deducted from these figures before they are used in your P&L. So for instance if I estimate month 2 as running at 25% capacity then I would expect treatment sales of £12,623 and product sales of £446.25. Less VAT, these figures would be:-

£12,623 ÷ 1.175 = £10,743
£446.25 ÷ 1.175 = £379.80

These will be the actual revenue amounts I would input into my example P&L for month 2.

  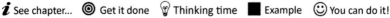

i See chapter... ◎ Get it done 💡 Thinking time ■ Example ☺ You can do it!

Profit & Loss	Month 1	Month 2	etc...	Totals = YEAR 1
Revenue	*at 10%*	*at 25%*		
Treatment sales (A)	?	?		
Product sales (B)	?	?		
Total Sales (A + B)	**£0.00**	**£0.00**		
Direct Costs				
Rent	?	?		
Salaries	?	?		
Stock	?	?		
License	?	?		
Total Direct Costs (C)	**£0.00**	**£0.00**		
Gross Profit (A+B-C)	**£0.00**	**£0.00**		
Gross Profit Percentage (GP/Sales)x100	?	?		
Indirect Costs (Overheads)				
MD/Owner salary	?	?		
Professional services *	?	?		
Website maintenance	?	?		
Loan repayments	?	?		
Bank fees	?	?		
Telephone Bills/Broadband	?	?		
Utilities	?	?		
Insurance	?	?		
Printing and Stationary	?	?		
Depreciation **	?	?		
Miscellaneous	?	?		
Total Indirect Costs (D)	**£0.00**	**£0.00**		
Net Profit (GP-D)	**£0.00**	**£0.00**		
Net Profit after Taxation				

Next, you will need to estimate your costs. Let's look at the direct costs first; the rent, salaries, stock and license.

Direct Costs:-

Once you have done the research into your market and premises, you should know what your direct costs will be. For this P&L example I will use the following direct costs:-

Rent = £12,000 per year
Staff Salaries = £7 per hour
Staff Commission = 10% of treatments
Stock = Estimate stock costs at 10% of sales
License = £800 per year (paid once a year)

With the above information, we need to work out the costs on a monthly basis.

Rent
Rent = 12,000 ÷ 12 = £1,000 per month

Salaries
These will need to be worked out in relation to the treatment revenue. So for instance in the 100% capacity treatment estimate, we said there were 6 money making stations fully booked for 8 hours. This requires at least 6 staff, plus 2 extra part-time to cover lunches and breaks, plus a receptionist; total 9 staff.

So in the following table, the 100% column shows how much 9 staff will cost a month:-

Salaries	at 100%	at 75%	at 50%	at 25%	at 10%
Daily client numbers	50	37.5	25	12.5	5
Daily sales	£1,980	£1,485	£990	£495	£198
Number of Staff needed to cover	9	7	5	3	2
Basis salaries @ £7 per hour + NIC*	£559.44	£419.58	£279.72	£186.48	£124.32
Commission @ 10% sales (after VAT)**	£168.51	£126.38	£84.26	£42.13	£16.85
Total Salaries per day	£728	£546	£364	£229	£141
Total Salaries per month (25.5 days)**	£18,563	£13,922	£9,281	£5,829	£3,600

* Remember NIC, national insurance contributions at approximately 11%; taking hourly rate to £7.77
**Remember to pay commission after you have deducted VAT
***Number of working days a month = 51 weeks x 6 days/week = 306 days ÷ 12 months = 25.5 days

9 staff x £7.77 per hour x 8 hours a day = £559.44 per day
Sales of £1,980 less VAT = 1980 ÷ 1.175 = £1,685.11
10% commission on sales after VAT = £1685.11 x 10% = £168.51

Therefore total salaries for a day = £559.44 + £168.51 = £728
Therefore total salaries for a month = £728 x 25.5 days = £18,563
The table then goes on to do the same calculations for all the other capacities.

---

 i See chapter... ◎ Get it done ♀ Thinking time ■ Example ☺ You can do it!

Stock

We can estimate stock costs at approximately 10% of treatment sales and at 40% of retail sales. Based on the previous revenue calculations, we can assess the following:-

At 100% capacity (shown in 2nd column), revenue is £1,980 and £70 for treatments and retail respectively. Therefore the estimated cost of stock needed to generate £1,980 will be = £1,980 x 10% = £198
The estimated cost of stock sold will be = £70 x 40% = £28

Total cost of stock for the day is = £198 + £28 = £226
So the total cost of stock for a month = £226 x 25.5 days = £5,763

As shown in the table below, do the same calculations for all the other capacities.

Stock	at 100%	at 75%	at 50%	at 25%	at 10%
Daily treatment sales	£1,980	£1,485	£990	£495	£198
Daily products sold	£70.00	£52.50	£35.00	£17.50	£7.00
Treatment stock usage @ 10% of sales	£198	£149	£99	£50	£20
Retail stock @ 40% of sales	£28	£21	£14	£7	£3
Total cost of stock per day	£226	£170	£113	£57	£23
Total cost of stock per month	£5,763	£4,322	£2,882	£1,441	£576

We are now ready to fill in the '?' gaps in our P&L and see what the Gross Profit and Gross Profit Percentage will be. I have estimated that in the first month of trading the salon will function at 10% of its capacity and at 25% in the second month.

However, please note that shown in the following table, trading at 10% is actually a loss making capacity with 2 staff working. If you reduce staff to 1 person, then the salary at this capacity will reduce to £2,014.78 (or £2,015) :-

Profit & Loss	Month 1	Month 2	etc...	Totals = YEAR 1
Revenue	*at 10%*	*at 25%*		
Treatment sales (A)	£4,297.02	£10,742.55		
Product sales (B)	£151.91	£379.79		
Total Sales (A + B)	**£4,448.94**	**£11,122.34**		
Direct Costs				
Rent	£1,000.00	£1,000.00		
Salaries	£3,599.86	£5,829.50		
Stock	£576.30	£1,440.75		
License	£0.00	£0.00		
Total Direct Costs (C)	**£5,176.16**	**£8,270.25**		
Gross Profit (A+B-C)	**-£727.23**	**£2,852.10**		
Gross Profit Percentage (GP/Sales)x100	-16%	26%		

Salaries	at 100%	at 75%	at 50%	at 25%	at 10%
Daily client numbers	50	37.5	25	12.5	5
Daily sales	£1,980	£1,485	£990	£495	£198
Number of Staff needed to cover	9	7	5	3	1
Basis salaries @ £7 per hour + NIC*	£559.44	£419.58	£279.72	£186.48	£62.16
Commission @ 10% sales (after VAT)**	£168.51	£126.38	£84.26	£42.13	£16.85
Total Salaries per day	£728	£546	£364	£229	£79
Total Salaries per month (25.5 days)**	£18,563	£13,922	£9,281	£5,829	£2,015

Putting the new salary into the P&L shows the 10% capacity becoming profitable (see P&L table on the next page), however this means 1 person seeing 5 customers a day, 6 days a week. This would be too much for most employees. The solution would be to have someone do a part-time shift to assist. If someone came for a third of the time, i.e., 16 hours a week the total salary cost would be £2,490 and you would still make a gross profit of approximately £400. (I calculated this by putting 1.3 as my number of staff in the salary calculations).

 i See chapter... ◎ Get it done ♀ Thinking time ■ Example ☺ You can do it!

Profit & Loss	Month 1	Month 2	etc...	Totals = YEAR 1
Revenue	at 10%	at 25%		
Treatment sales (A)	£4,297.02	£10,742.55		
Product sales (B)	£151.91	£379.79		
Total Sales (A + B)	**£4,448.94**	**£11,122.34**		
Direct Costs				
Rent	£1,000.00	£1,000.00		
Salaries	£2,014.78	£5,829.50		
Stock	£576.30	£1,440.75		
License	£0.00	£0.00		
Total Direct Costs (C)	**£3,591.08**	**£8,270.25**		
Gross Profit (A+B-C)	**£857.85**	**£2,852.10**		
Gross Profit Percentage (GP/Sales)x100	19%	26%		

Please note, I have put £0 for the license because in this case it is a yearly fee and would have been paid for from the capital, just like the chairs and tables.

Now we need to look at the Indirect Costs or business overheads.

Indirect Costs / Overheads:-
Looking at the list on page 233-234, you will need to guesstimate what you think your monthly overheads will be.

- MD/Owner salary
- Professional services
- Web site maintenance
- Loan repayments
- Bank fees
- Telephone Bills / Broadband
- Utilities
- Insurance

- Printing and stationery
- Depreciation**
- Miscellaneous (Staff outings, travel, fines, penalties, etc)

Unlike direct costs there is no way of calculating them based on sales as indirect costs are not directly related to sales... hence the name indirect! I will use some fictional figures for the P&L example but you will need to estimate yours from the research you do, taking into consideration your particular circumstances. Please be as realistic about these numbers as you can, underestimate and you may end-up shocked when you can't pay your bills! Obviously if your overheads are too high, causing financial strain on the business, you will have to look into how you can reduce them from the start.

So for the purpose of my P&L example I will estimate the following indirect costs:-

Overheads	Yearly	Quarterly	Monthly
MD/Owner Salary *	£10,000.00	£2,500.00	£833.33
Professional services **	£800.00	£200.00	£66.67
Website maintenance	£300.00	£75.00	£25.00
Loan repayments	£3,000.00	£750.00	£250.00
Bank fees	£180.00	£45.00	£15.00
Telephone Bills/Broadband	£700.00	£175.00	£58.33
Utilities	£1,800.00	£450.00	£150.00
Insurance	£1,200.00	£300.00	£100.00
Printing and Stationary	£700.00	£175.00	£58.33
Depreciation ***	£4,000.00	£1,000.00	£333.33
Miscellaneous	£2,400.00	£600.00	£200.00
Total Overheads	**£25,080.00**	**£6,270.00**	**£2,090.00**

* Put owners low because working part-time in salon

** mainly accountant

*** capital spend on salon fixtures, fittings and equipment was £20,000; expect most of the items to last 5 years. Therefore depreciation rate at £4,000 per year.

Note:- Not all bills will be paid on a monthly basis.

i See chapter...   ◎ Get it done   ♀ Thinking time   ■ Example   ☺ You can do it!

Adding these overhead costs to the P&L forecast reveals the net profit situation:-

Profit & Loss	Month 1	Month 2	etc...	Totals = YEAR 1
Revenue	**at 10%**	**at 25%**		
Treatment sales (A)	£4,297.02	£10,742.55		
Product sales (B)	£151.91	£379.79		
Total Sales (A + B)	**£4,448.94**	**£11,122.34**		
Direct Costs				
Rent	£1,000.00	£1,000.00		
Salaries	£2,490.31	£5,829.50		
Stock	£576.30	£1,440.75		
License	£0.00	£0.00		
Total Direct Costs (C)	**£4,066.61**	**£8,270.25**		
Gross Profit (A+B-C)	**£382.33**	**£2,852.10**		
Gross Profit Percentage (GP/Sales)x100	9%	26%		
Indirect Costs (Overheads)				
MD/Owner salary	£833.33	£833.33		
Professional services *	£0.00	£0.00		
Website maintenance	£25.00	£25.00		
Loan repayments	£250.00	£250.00		
Bank fees	£15.00	£15.00		
Telephone Bills/Broadband	£58.33	£58.33		
Utilities	£0.00	£0.00		
Insurance	£100.00	£100.00		
Printing and Stationary	£0.00	£0.00		
Depreciation **	£333.33	£333.33		
Miscellaneous	£0.00	£200.00		
Total Indirect Costs (D)	**£1,615.00**	**£1,815.00**		
Net Profit (GP-D)	**-£1,232.67**	**£1,037.10**		
Net Profit after Taxation				

I haven't paid professional fees, as I think there won't be any in the first few months. Utilities are usually paid quarterly. Most of the printing and stationery would have been done and purchased as part of the capital spend and expected to last a few months.

The Net Profit after Taxation row doesn't need to be calculated on a monthly basis; once a year will do as profits are usually declared yearly, allowing you to take into account any losses in the same year.

Completing And Presenting The P&L Forecast

Now that we have covered the first 2 months of a P&L, start to produce your own P&L forecast, completing all the monthly columns to show a full 3 years forecast. For your business plan you will need to display this information in both a monthly and yearly format.

The summarised yearly format should look like this:-

3 year Profit & Loss forecast	Year 1	Year 2	Year 3
Revenue	£302,940.00	£454,410.00	£554,410.00
Direct Costs	£240,000.00	£345,000.00	£400,000.00
Gross Profit	**£62,940.00**	**£109,410.00**	**£154,410.00**
GPP	21%	24%	28%
Indirect Costs (Overheads)	£25,000.00	£30,000.00	£43,000.00
Net Profit	**£37,940.00**	**£79,410.00**	**£111,410.00**
Net Profit after Taxation			

Your P&L is now complete!

Showing Your Calculations And Assumptions

In the above example I have stated my calculations and assumptions along the way. For example with the small notes under the tables saying the number of working weeks in a year or how the depreciation was calculated. Ideally these should all be consolidated onto one

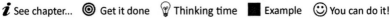

sheet, entitled Calculations and Assumptions so that readers can easily find all the information they need about how you came about the figures that you've used.

The Breakeven Point

This is the point when your sales revenue makes neither a profit nor a loss. The breakeven point can be calculated using the following formula:-

Overheads ÷ GPP = Breakeven Point

Using the previous figures from Year 1, the breakeven point is = £25,000 ÷ 21% ≈ £119,000

So breakeven will be achieved when sales reach £119,000.

The breakeven analysis needs to be included in your business plan.

Setting Sales Targets

Your daily, weekly, monthly and yearly sales targets should be set directly from your Revenue Forecasts and Profit & Loss estimates. Once you have done your revenue forecast calculations, as shown on pages 235 – 237, and input this information into your P&L estimates as shown on page 253, then to set your sales targets, all you need to do is convert this information into the appropriate time-frames. So if you want daily targets for month 1, then divide the sales estimate for that month by the number of trading days in that month... and so on.

The Balance Sheet

A balance sheet is the statement of the total assets and liabilities of a business on a particular date, also showing its total net worth.

How does what the business owns balance against what the business owes?

Net worth = Assets - Liabilities
Is the business' net worth negative or positive?

The balance sheet is different from a P&L or Cash flow statement as it is usually a one-pager that will show, at a glance, the company's state of affairs. Just think, the P&L and Cash flow statements don't total and show all the assets, debts or type of debts the business has.

A balance sheet should consists of fixed assets, current assets, long-term debts and current or short-term debts. You should have your accountant prepare the balance sheet at least once a year.

Some balance sheet observations:-

- Ideally you want the balance sheet to show that the value of the businesses assets is greater than its total liabilities. It isn't a huge problem if this isn't the case, especially if the debts are short-term and cash flow is positive. If the debts are short-term and cash flow is low then this may indicate that you could have problems paying your creditors on time.

- If one of the fixed assets listed is your shop-fit (fixtures and fittings), remember that this will depreciate in value as time goes on; it's not a positive outlook if you have loans that extend for much longer than the lifespan of this asset.

- On your balance sheet, it is better to have decent medium to long-term loans as your liabilities than unpaid supplier's invoices, due tax payments, maxed-out overdrafts and other current liabilities that could potentially see the business in court! These types of creditors could demand payment at any time which is a threat to the business.

FINANCIAL FORECASTS SECTION SUMMARY

One thing I really want you to understand here is that producing financial forecasts isn't just for when you want to raise money and need a business plan, they are very important for you! Well thought-out and researched P&L and Cash flow forecasts will not only clearly indicate whether your business idea is viable, i.e., has the potential to actually work and is worth pursuing! But will also help you:-

- Know your costs
- Set your prices
- Set the business clear financial objectives and milestones
- Prepare daily sales targets to keep your salon on track and motivate the team
- Be less vulnerable to crisis management; understanding your businesses potential weak areas and limitations
- Estimate and source contingency money; at least 3 – 6 months worth

Now that the financial forecasts section is complete we can look at other general areas of accounting...

OTHER AREAS IN FINANCE

Accounting

Unless you are a trained accountant or very competent with numbers, most of your "important accounting" should be handled by an accountant. When I say important, I mean any information that needs to be presented to the Inland Revenue, Companies House or shareholders. However, preparing P&L and cash flow forecasts should be done by you as you need to create, know and understand your businesses finances and financial objectives.

Important accounting:-

- Paying wages; payslips, P45's, P60's, PAYE
- Paying yourself; as above plus Self Assessment Returns
- VAT returns
- PAYE calculations
- Self assessment tax returns
- Partnership tax returns
- Bookkeeping
- End of year P&L accounts
- Corporation tax
- Balance sheet
- Paying dividends

DIY accounting:-

- Paying bills and invoices
- Preparing salary information
- Updating P&L forecast
- Updating cash flow forecast
- Keeping clear and complete spending records; receipts and invoice records
- Cashing up and recording revenue

---

 i See chapter... ◎ Get it done 💡 Thinking time ■ Example ☺ You can do it!

Management Accounts

Management accounts are just the financial documents you keep and update to help you monitor and stay in control of your business. For example, the cash flow would be one of your management accounting tools. All of the above DIY accounting items are all part of your management accounts.

There's more on your daily accounting tasks in the section on Financials in *i* chapter 11, On-Going Management.

Business Bank Account

I strongly advise that you have a separate bank account for your business transactions. Most banks offer business bank accounts. The information required to open a company account verses a sole trader account is different. You have to have registered your company with Companies House before you can open a business account for this company.

If you have a good, long-standing relationship with the bank holding your personal account, you may find it easy and convenient to stick with them when opening your business account. However, all banks are eager for new business; visit a few, collect their info packs for business accounts and choose one!

VAT (Value Added Tax)

VAT is the tax added to taxable products and services. This is usually at a rate of 17.5% in the UK. At present, you do not have to register your business for VAT until it reaches a turnover of £64,000 in one year. If you are registered then your VAT calculations and returns are very important to get right for your business, as the taxman doesn't play around with this!

First there is the VAT you pay when you purchase salon supplies and other items; you claim this back. Then there is the VAT you charge when you provide services and sell products; you pay this to the taxman.

Example

You buy £300 worth of products for your business. You pay your supplier £300 + VAT = £300 + (£300 x 17.5%) = £300 + £52.50 = £352.50
If your business is VAT registered you claim the £52.50 VAT back.

Say you sell 5 facials at £60 each. As a VAT registered company your clients have paid for the facial plus VAT within that £60. The VAT that they have paid you as part of the £60 belongs to the Inland Revenue.

Just as your supplier has to pay that £52.50 to the Inland Revenue, you also have to pay them any VAT you charge your clients.

Basically VAT is a tax you collect on behalf of the Inland Revenue and you must not include this money in your thoughts! To workout how much VAT you have collected on each £60 your clients paid, do the following calculation:-

£60 ÷ 1.175 = **£51.06 This is the actual price of your facial and the money that belongs to the business**

£60 - £51.06 = **£8.94 This is the VAT you charged per facial**

For the 5 facials totalling £300 in sales, your business collected £8.94 x 5 = £44.70 in VAT

If your business is VAT registered you pay the £44.70 VAT to the Inland Revenue.

Back to the beginning...

i See chapter...   ◎ Get it done   ⚲ Thinking time   ■ Example   ☺ You can do it!

You bought stock worth £300 and paid VAT of £52.50 to the supplier, which you have to claim back from the Inland Revenue; You sold stock worth £300 and collected £44.70 VAT which you have to handover to the Inland Revenue.

Your VAT Return will therefore show that the taxman owes you:-
£52.50 - £44.70 = £7.80

OR
If you did 10 facials totalling £600 with VAT charged totalling £89.40 Your VAT Return will show that you owe the taxman:-
£89.40 - £52.50 = £36.90

That's VAT in a nutshell. In summary, make sure you keep all your receipts & invoices and really good records of all your sales; use them to keep track of what your VAT liability would be but ultimately hand these documents over to your accountant and have him/her calculate and complete your VAT Return for you!!

Corporation Tax

Corporation tax only applies to limited companies. If your company made a profit at the end of the accounting period, normally a 12 month period; that profit will be taxed at 20% (this rate is correct as at 2008 but may change; please see www.hmrc.gov.uk for current rates).

Paying Your Staff

Your staff salaries should be processed by your accountant or a payroll processing company, these people can also be referred to as your agents or representatives. Your job is to inform them how much each person has earned during the period and how it has been divided, i.e. how much commission, how much basic, how many days sick, holiday, etc. They will let you know how best to get this information to them. Also see chapter 7, Staff.

Your accountant or payroll processing company will deal with all matters of the Pay As You Earn (PAYE) system, employers and employees national insurance contributions (ER and EE NIC), P45's, P46's, tax codes, emergency tax codes, maternity pay and more!

If you would like to educate yourself on the meanings of all of these payroll aspects then visit www.businesslink.gov.uk and select Taxes, Returns and Payroll. Otherwise please let your appointed agents deal with these matters so that you can spend more time on things that they can't do for you, like marketing!

Just remember that after each payroll is processed your agent should provide you with the total tax and NIC's that you will need to pay over to HM Revenue & Customs (HMRC).

I strongly advice that you make these payments regularly and definitely on-time, as HMRC have the power to close your business down!

Also, if you don't pay, then you will technically have all this money in the business account that doesn't belong to the business anymore and in a cash flow crisis be tempted to use it, potentially getting yourself into bigger problems in the future! Take heed.

◎Put a row in your cash flow dedicated to tax in all its forms.

PAYE Scheme (Pay As You Earn)

The Pay As You Earn Scheme is the method used by HMRC to deduct Income Tax and National Insurance Contributions (NIC) from your employees and directors (if limited company) wages. So with every payslip, IT and NIC are deducted from each employees total pay;

these amounts, as mentioned before, need to be handed over to the taxman. **Again, like VAT, this is money that will be in your business bank account but does not belong to you or the business and as such you need to be very good at NOT SPENDING IT!** As an employer you will be responsible for calculating and sending these amounts to the Inland Revenue on a monthly or quarterly basis; late or incorrect payments are subject to fines. The company or accountant that you hire to handle your payroll and produce payslips will automatically do these calculations for you and even make the payments... this, I think, is the best option! See more on PAYE at www.businesslink.gov. uk and www.hmrc.gov.uk

Paying Your Own Wages

How you pay yourself depends on your businesses structure. If you are a sole trader or partnership then you will probably draw a set amount of money from the business on a monthly basis, keep a record of these drawings, then inform your accountant of the total amount and have him/her complete your Self Assessment tax returns for you once a year. You will then need to pay all the tax due for the year in one lump sum (!). Put money aside for this regularly so that when the bill comes you won't be too shocked and unprepared.

If you are a director of a limited company then you are considered an employee of the company and your pay will need to be processed in the same way all company employees are paid. This would mean you pay your tax regularly like all the other staff through the PAYE scheme. There are a few differences when paying company directors, but your accountant should handle those.

Again, don't play around with the tax payments. Remember that the cash no longer belongs to the business or company but HMRC and it is your sole responsibility, to see that it is paid.

Also, your earnings should be fair and affordable to the business! As the owner or a shareholder, you will make more money eventually when the business makes a profit and you pay out dividends. So be patient; you may need to sacrifice in the beginning to help grow your business.

Personal Tax (Self-Assessment)

If you choose the sole trader and/or partnership route then you are classed as self-employed and your personal tax returns will need to be completed once a year. Even as a company director, paying tax through the PAYE scheme, you may still need to complete a self-assessment tax return.

These tax forms are not that difficult to complete, however, as you will already have an accountant doing other work for your business, you might as well have them take care of this as well.

Paying Business Bills And Invoices

As previously discussed in *i* chapter 11, On-Going Management and above, paying business bills and invoices is a DIY accounting task. Keep an updated list of all bills and invoices and their due dates; mark these dates on your working calendar.

Once paid batch all receipts and invoices in order of type and date. For instance, all utility bills should be kept together; all stock invoices should be kept together and so on. These should then be batched under the month they were issued; this makes updating your P&L a hundred times easier!

Profit Sharing! - Return On Investment (ROI)

Well this is what it's all about! You invest time, effort and money in a business in order to get a Return On Investment (ROI)!

Profit distribution in a sole trader or partnership business is done in accordance with your written agreement.

Paying out profits to shareholders in a company setting is known as dividends. The dividend is the amount, usually expressed as a percentage of share value, of company profits that is distributed to its shareholders. Your accountant should handle any dividend calculations and payouts.

Remember that when your company or business makes a profit, it may not be wise to hand out all of the profits. As a director and/ or manager you should have a plan for the businesses future and as such may want to re-invest some of that money back into the business to grow it further.

Profits are not always for distribution but also very important for growth and rainy days.

So, congratulations but don't spend it all at once!

Chapter Summary

Having financial control is vital for the success of your business. The businesses cash flow, profit & loss and balance sheet statements will provide a complete overview of the businesses money situation. This is important not just for you and your management of the business but also vitally important to the bank, your business partners, the taxman and any investors or shareholders you have.

Chapter 15
HEALTH & SAFETY, LICENSING AND INSURANCE

Health and Safety (H&S)

What Is H&S And How Does It Relate To Your Salon Business?

Any responsible business owner would want to ensure that they are providing their staff with a safe working environment. As such ensuring the H&S of your staff, customers and any other users of your premises during trading hours is an important aspect of running your own company.

If you employ 5 or more staff you are required by law to have a written H&S policy which your staff will need to be aware of.

However, if you employ less than 5 staff, I recommend that you still have clear H&S policies and procedures.

◎ In the UK, to cover your H&S responsibilities you will need:-

- A Health & Safety Policy
- A Health & Safety Procedure Manual
- To display the Health & Safety Law poster in your salon (this poster can be purchased from the HSE web site for £6.38, see end of section for details)

Let's look at how to prepare these documents in detail...

Bear in mind though, that because every salon is different it would be impossible for me to write your procedure manual for you; as such the following information is a guide, full of examples, on what is important and relevant to salons in terms of H&S!

THE SALON'S WRITTEN HEALTH & SAFETY POLICY AND PROCEDURE MANUAL

The H&S Policy should contain the following:-

1. The company's general statement of intent
2. Arrangements for the implementation of the safety policy
3. Organisation responsibilities

The H&S procedure manual should address the following areas:-

1. Risk Assessments; including safety and best practice assessment for every salon process/treatment
2. Induction training; ensuring all staff understand the H&S procedures and their roles
3. The salon's environmental conditions; lighting, cleanliness, ventilation, etc
4. Storage
5. Electrical equipment
6. First Aid
7. Workplace ergonomics; ensuring equipment, furniture and tools are designed for maximum comfort, safety and ease of use
8. Hazardous substances; COSHH for every chemical used
9. Fire safety and emergency evacuation
10. Accident and incident reporting

Let's look at all of the above in some detail...

If you're struggling with this, remember you can buy ready-made H&S Policy, Procedure and Induction templates from www.misssalonbusiness.com

---

The H&S Policy

1. The company's general statement of intent

This is basically where you as the owner or managing director make a statement about the businesses attitude towards H&S and its aims and objectives around H&S.

2. Arrangements for the implementation of the safety policy

Here you will need to outline the levels of responsibility and general processes and methods by which you and your team will go about ensuring that the salon's H&S procedures are in operation.

3. Organisational responsibilities

In this section you should go into a detailed list of all the levels of employee H&S responsibilities. For example, below is a list of an MD's or owners H&S responsibility. You will need to create similar lists for the operations manager, the actual salon manager, beauty therapist, nail technician, hairdresser, etc. Every type of role will have a different level of responsibility.

■ **For example,** the Managing Directors or Owners list of responsibilities could be as follows:-

- To establish the *[Insert name of your business]* Health and Safety Policy and to cause it to be reviewed and revised as often as is necessary, being at maximum intervals of 12 months;

- To allocate the necessary resources to ensure that the requirements of the policy can be fulfilled;

- To liaise with the Landlord with regard to matters of mutual concern;

- Monitor the effectiveness of the Policy;

- To be aware of the statutory health and safety requirements sufficient to discharge these duties;

- To discuss any actions required with regard to health and safety concerns brought to her/his attention by any line manager or *[Insert employee work title; nail technician, therapist, hairdresser, etc]*

- Support at all times the intent of the Policy to secure the safety and health of employees, clients and other users of the premises;

- Set a personal example at all times.

The H&S Procedure Manual

1. Risk Assessments
The aim of a salon risk assessment is to produce a list that identifies all the potential hazards in the salon and clear procedures on how to prevent and handle them effectively.

◎ Create your salon's risk assessment by going through the salon and every salon operation; from cleaning to treatments; identifying any potential hazards. Hazards may be anything from loose wires, spills and hot table-lamp bulbs, to sharp edges on work stations, lack of proper ventilation and loose floor tiles. Once you have created a complete list, proceed to then outline how these hazards can be avoided and if a problem does arise, how it should be handled.

Some examples of areas to think about when conducting your risk assessment are:-

- Handling of chemicals
- Disposal of materials
- Storage of materials
- Workplace ergonomics
- Occupational skin disease
- Working environment
- Electrical equipment

- Emergency procedures

■ **For example**
Under the area of 'HANDLING OF CHEMICALS', one of the observations in a nail salon would be as follows:-

Risk:-
During the transfer of acetone from a 5 litre container to 100ml station pumps there may be spills of acetone. Excessive spillage of acetone can cause damage to property, furniture and stock. See COSHH on Acetone for more on damage caused by excessive exposure to Acetone.

Procedure:-
Acetone is a highly flammable liquid and the 5 litre containers must be stored in the fire cabinet. Transfers must only be done on a flat surface using a funnel, whilst wearing gloves and protective glasses. Also there must be plenty of paper towels at hand to mop up any spills. The 100ml station pump must be labelled as containing a 100ml of Acetone.

■ **Another example**
Under the area of 'OCCUPATIONAL SKIN DISEASE', one of the observations would be as follows:-

Risk:-
Because of the nature of the treatments offered in the salon an operators hands may be overexposed to water and detergents; for example, during hair washing and treating, pedicures, cleaning etc. This can eventually lead to contact dermatitis.

Procedure:-
Whenever appropriate the operator should protect hands by wearing disposable gloves. Also, as often as possible, they should apply a light, fragrance-free, moisturising cream to the hands and nails.

2. Induction Training

H&S induction training should be given to all new staff. Your induction training should consist of all the important and relevant aspects of safety and health in their daily working activities. Even though all this important information maybe in their staff handbook, it is your responsibility as an employer to ensure that they know how to stay safe at work.

◎ Create your H&S induction training agenda by consolidating the most pertinent information from your H&S Procedure manual. The training should take about an hour (depending on the size of your business) and should include practical and visual examples of the salon's safe practises.

Remember to include in the training material:-

- The agenda, the actual safety processes and what to do in case of this and that;
- Date and location of training (location should be in the salon);
- Name of trainer;
- Name of trainee and signature (a declaration).

Give every trainee a copy of all the details of the training they have just received.

You can purchase a sample of a complete H&S Induction Training programme used in a real salon for £9.99 from www.misssalon. com

3. The Salon's Environmental Conditions

The salon's environmental conditions include cleanliness, temperature, ventilation, lighting and refuse. ◎ In this H&S procedure manual clearly state the salon's policies on and methods of maintaining all of the above.

In the cleanliness section in particular, include how the treatment areas should be prepared and maintained for maximum hygiene and safety. Will you use a cleaning company? Who will clean the WC, showers, sinks, skirting boards, floors, windows, outdoor sign, etc? What about the towels? The daily use of disinfectants and antibacterial sprays along with disposable clothes and paper towels is advised. Your salon should be spotless!

A well ventilated salon is very important, particularly when working with odorous chemicals such as acrylics, nail polish, hairsprays, etc. See that you address this properly in the design of your salon; you may want to consult with the H&S licensing officer when making your shop-fit plans (see later section on Licensing).

The temperature in workrooms should normally be at least 16 degrees Celsius; this may vary in a salon depending on the treatments and treatment areas. In general, the law states that during working hours, the temperature in all workplaces inside buildings shall be reasonable; that is, providing reasonable comfort without the need for special clothing.

4. Storage
◎In this section you should outline the various storage places and systems in the salon. Particular attention should be paid to the labelling, storage and handling of highly flammable liquids.

5. Electrical Equipment
All the electrical equipment in your salon must be checked and certified as fit for use. Most brand-new electrical equipment does not need checking for at least a year, but this may not be the case for all items.

The Health and Safety Executive (HSE) advise the following:-

You can find out if your electrical equipment is safe by carrying out suitable checks, such as inspection and/or testing. The level of inspection and/or testing should depend upon the risks. A simple visual inspection is likely to be sufficient for equipment used in a clean dry environment.

A simple visual inspection, as described by the HSE, consists of the following:-

- Switch off and unplug the equipment before you start any checks.
- Check that the plug is correctly wired (but only if you are competent to do so).
- Ensure the fuse is correctly rated by checking the equipment rating plate or instruction book.
- Check that the plug is not damaged and that the cable is properly secured with no internal wires visible.
- Check the electrical cable is not damaged and has not been repaired with insulating tape or an unsuitable connector. Damaged cable should be replaced with a new cable by a competent person.
- Check that the outer cover of the equipment is not damaged in a way that will give rise to electrical or mechanical hazards.
- Check for burn marks or staining that suggests the equipment is overheating.
- Position any trailing wires so that they are not a trip hazard and are less likely to get damaged.

I think for peace of mind and best practice you should have an electrician do a once-over on all the electrical equipment from the start and keep this practice going once a year. He can also advise you on which salon equipment may need extra attention.

◉ For the purpose of your H&S manual, make a statement about the level of risk associated with the electrical equipment used in your salon; is it high or low risk equipment? It's most probably low risk as most salon equipment is used in clean dry environments.

Next, list the salons electrical equipment and what level of checks they require, who will do those checks and when. Highlight what you are looking for when doing your visual checks. Keep a record of the

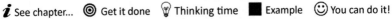

condition of all equipment and when last inspected.

The table below gives a list of suggested initial inspection intervals for different types of equipment:-

Type of business	User checks	Formal visual inspection	Electrician inspection
Office information technology eg desktop computers, photocopiers, fax machines	No	1 to 2 years	None if double-insulated otherwise up to 5 years
Double insulated equipment not hand-held, eg fans, table lamps	No	2 to 3 years	No
Hand-held double insulated (Class II) equipment, eg some floor cleaners, kitchen equipment and irons	Yes	6 months to 1 year	No
Earthed (Class I) equipment, eg electric kettles, some floor cleaners	Yes	6 months to 1 year	1 to 2 years
Equipment used by the public, eg in hotels	By member of staff	3 months	1 year
Cables and plugs, extension leads	Yes	1 year	2 years

6. First Aid

Once you have completed your risk assessments you will be able to decide what level of first aid is required in your salon and whether your premises needs a trained first aider. Most salons do not need a trained first aider as generally speaking the risks to safety and health are low. You will however definitely need to appoint a responsible person to take charge in case of an accident or emergency. Whoever is appointed for the job needs to be made known to the rest of the team and have a deputy in case of their absence.

◉ Your manual should include the first aider(s), the location of the first aid box and the location of the accident book/log. Any first aid treatment (using plasters, bandages, sterile wipes) to a minor accident, received by an employee or client must be recorded in the accident log.

Steer clear of storing any medication in the first aid box; even ordinary pain killers. No one other than a fully trained and qualified first aider should administer any treatments.

In a serious emergency, do as you would at home, call an ambulance!

If you feel you need or should have a trained first aider on site then you or an appointed employee can take a training course in first aid at work. Find local HSE (Health and Safety Executive) approved courses and trainers on their web site; www.hse.gov.uk

First Aid Kits can be purchased from some beauty industry suppliers, but there are many companies online that retail this product. Type 'first aid kits' into Google and take your pick!

You must have a first aid box in your salon.

7. Workplace Ergonomics
◎ In this section you should discuss the furniture and design of the salon; the risks of musculoskeletal disorders and how your setup and procedures help to prevent that. For example, are the work trolleys the right height to minimise bending; are the therapists seats height adjustable to ensure comfort during facials; do you provide or advise special footwear to assist with standing for long periods, etc.

This is also the section where you should discuss fatigue prevention techniques, such as the frequency of staff 'tea' breaks and other changes in activity.

8. Hazardous Substances
Firstly, as most salon products and substances are designed to be

used on skin, nails and hair, they are not regarded as presenting major health risks. However, it is recognised that prolonged exposure can result in chronic conditions of the skin (e.g. dermatitis) and respiratory tract. As such, most salon products, if not all, are supplied with Material Safety Data Sheets (MSDS) or Control of Substances Hazardous to Health (COSHH) sheets; these sheets provide detailed product information and guidance on best practice.

These safety data sheets generally outline the following:-

- Name of product/substance;
- Define its risk factor; toxic, corrosive, etc;
- What container it is in;
- Who is exposed to it and for how long;
- Effects on health;
- Storage arrangements;
- Handling arrangements;
- Control methods;
- Emergency arrangements.

Any reputable manufacturer will supply their products with one of these safe-use documents; though you may still need to complete a COSHH sheet for ones that don't.

Also check out www.coshh-essentials.org.uk

A substance hazardous to health means any substance (including preparation) which is:-

- Any substance which is classified and labelled as very toxic, toxic, harmful, corrosive or irritant. The packaging or containers holding such a substance will bear a label which will have a black symbol on an orange background with the appropriate warning printed below;
- A substance for which a maximum exposure limit or an occupational exposure standard is specified in HSE guidance note EH40;
- A biological agent;

- Dusts of any kind, when present at a substantial concentration in the air;
- Any substance which has similar properties to the foregoing.

◎ For your H&S Procedures manual make a complete list of all hazardous substances in use in the salon and in what processes/treatments they are used; include who maintains this list and where it is kept. Keep the risk assessments on those particular substances and processes together with this list, along with their MSDS or COSHH sheets.

As explained earlier in the Risk Assessment section, the risk assessments would already include procedures to control the possible dangers of overexposure to these substances; however, in your manual, you should again add 'general methods' to keep exposure under control. For example, the use of personal protective equipment, limiting the time spent exposed, etc.

☺ This may all seem a little complicated but just be cool and use your common sense; it's not that hard once you get started. Even if you don't think you have everything perfectly laid out; just remember that ultimately the most important thing is to ensure that you and your team are equipped, know what to do in an emergency and how to stay safe at work!

9. Fire Safety And Emergency Evacuations
◎ In this section you will need to outline the following:-

- The means of escape and fire assembly points;
- Maintenance of the fire fighting equipment and their exact locations;
- The training given to all employees on the location and use of all fire fighting equipment, as well as the means of escape; including fire drills;
- Fire drills;
- A list of actions to be taken on discovering a fire;
- A list of actions to be taken on hearing a fire alarm;

---

i See chapter...   ◎ Get it done   ♀ Thinking time   ■ Example   ☺ You can do it!

- The No-Smoking policy;
- Other instructions such as:-
  - At no time is fire fighting equipment and fire alarms to be obstructed;
  - Any person who has to discharge a fire extinguisher to combat a fire should report the matter to the Manager who will arrange to have the extinguisher recharged or replaced.

Fire Extinguishers
Fire fighting equipment must be maintained at least once a year and recharged or replaced after use. There are different fire extinguishers for fires burning on different substances. Make sure you have and use the appropriate fire extinguisher for the type of fire.

My advice...

Have a fire safety officer visit your salon, assess the fire risks and recommend an evacuation procedure and the correct fire fighting equipment. This should cost no more than £300 including the equipment. Worth the money I reckon!

Speak to your local boroughs H&S department; they normally provide advice and training for employers, businesses and employees and the self-employed. Ask them to recommend a local fire consultant or to inspect your premises and give their advice.

Remember most salons have lots of electrical equipment, high potential for spills and splashes and a fair amount of flammable liquids; check your equipment regularly, clean up spills and splashes immediately and store all flammables in a fire cabinet!!!

10. Accident And Incident Reporting
The requirement for the formal notification of accidents to the

enforcement authorities is contained in The Reporting of Injuries, Diseases and Dangerous Occurrences Regulations 1995 (RIDDOR).

The following documents are required to be available for compliance with this procedure:-

- BI510 Accident Book; available to purchase for £4.75+VAT from HSE Books or other good bookshops

- Your Salons Accident and Incident Report Form; a form briefly documenting:-
  - WHO: Name, address, age and gender of the injured person. Are they employees or member of the public?
  - WHAT: Find out what has happened, do not speculate; stick to known facts
  - WHERE: Precise location of the accident
  - WHEN: Time/date of the injured parties

- Form 2508 (01/96) Report of an injury or dangerous occurrence

- Form 2508A (01/96) Report of a case of disease

The last two forms can be replaced by a simple phone call to the ICC (Incident Contact Centre) on 0845 300 99 23 or by completing the forms online. Find these and more information on RIDDOR on the HSE web site; www.hse.gov.uk/riddor

In most cases reporting to the ICC is not necessary, but if you are ever in doubt, telephone them and find out. Information supplied to HSE in a RIDDOR report is not passed on to your insurance company. If required, you will need to contact your insurance company separately.

Incidences you should report to the ICC

As an employer, a person who is self-employed, or someone in control of work premises, you have legal duties under RIDDOR that require you to report and record some work-related accidents by the quickest means possible.

You must report:-

- Deaths;
- Major injuries; amputations, dislocations, fractures, temporary loss of sight, electric shock, burns to the eyes, etc. See full list on HSE web site given above
- Over-3-day injuries – where an employee or self-employed person is away from work or unable to perform their normal work duties for more than 3 consecutive days;
- Injuries to members of the public or people not at work where they are taken from the scene of an accident to hospital;
- Some work-related diseases;
- Dangerous occurrences – where something happens that does not result in an injury, but could have done;

In both cases of reportable and non-reportable incidents the B1510 accident book and your salons incident and accident form should be completed.

◎ In your H&S manual state the above and the location of the accident book and forms, all the relevant phone numbers and who is in charge of the reporting procedures.

Accident prevention
The prevention of accidents is something that's handled in your risk assessments. So for example the risks of slips, trips and falls will be minimised if your risk assessment procedure included the following recommendations:-

- Keep the salon clean, tidy, congestion-free and well lit
- Clear up spillage promptly and post warning notices
- Repair or replace damaged floor coverings immediately, especially on stairways and areas where the public have access
- Keep a clearly marked first-aid kit available at all times

That's the written H&S Policy and Procedures Manual completed! PHEW!

Health & Safety - THE LAW

The following information has been directly sourced from the Health and Safety Executive (HSE).

The Health and Safety at Work etc Act 1974 requires you to provide whatever information, instruction, training and supervision as is necessary to ensure, so far as is reasonably practicable, the health and safety at work of your employees.

This is expanded by the Management of Health and Safety at Work Regulations 1999, which identify situations where health and safety training is particularly important, e.g. when people start work, on exposure to new or increased risks and where existing skills may have become rusty or need updating.

You must provide training during working hours and not at the expense of your employees. Special arrangements may be needed for part-timers or shift workers.

You need to assess the risks to your employees while they are at work and to any other people who may be affected by the way you conduct your business. This is so that you can identify the measures you need to take to comply with health and safety law, which includes training and the provision of information.

Like many employers, you may not be in a position to provide this training on your own, in which case you will need competent help. If at all possible, you should appoint one or more of your employees. However, if there is no one with the relevant knowledge, experience and skills in your organisation who can be relied on to deal effectively with health and safety training, you need to enlist someone who has from outside. In some circumstances you may need a combination

of internal and external help. Look at www.businesslink.gov.uk. for detailed advice on choosing and managing a health and safety consultant.

The Safety Representatives and Safety Committees Regulations 1977 and the Health and Safety (Consultation with Employees) Regulations 1996 require you to consult your employees, or their representatives, on health and safety issues.

Representatives appointed under either of these sets of regulations are entitled to time off with pay for training in their duties. The Health and Safety (Training for Employment) Regulations 1990 ensure that learners doing work experience are covered by health and safety law.

What about self-employed people?
If a person working under your control and direction is treated as self-employed for tax and national insurance purposes, they may nevertheless be treated as your employee for health and safety purposes. You may need therefore to take appropriate action to protect them.

[This information has been directly sourced from the HSE]

Where To Find More Information And Assistance?

- www.coshh-essentials.org.uk – COSHH Essentials; use this site to assess the risk of each chemical used in a treatment and a control approach.

- www.hse.gov.uk – this is the web site of the Health and Safety Executive. Type in 'beauty salon' or 'nail bar' into their search and you can find plenty of very useful H&S information. Also try www.hsebooks.co.uk for the HSE priced and free publications.

- www.learndirect.co.uk will help you find health and safety

training courses

- I found a very useful and simply presented guide to Risk Management in Hair and Beauty Salons on the insurers, MORE THAN BUSINESS, web site. Visit http://www.morethanbusiness.com/documents/16/HairdressingBeautyRMG.pdf

- www.businesslink.gov.uk select Health, Safety, Premises.

> You can also buy a fully prepared salon H&S Policy template for £19.99 and a salon H&S Procedure template (with example entries) for £24.99 from www.misssalonbusiness.com

H&S Section Summary

The more thorough you are when preparing your risk assessments and H&S procedure manual the less likely you will run into problems in the future with accidents, licensing and inspections. Purchasing the H&S tools from Miss Salon will save you a lot of time and uncertainty, but you and your team will still need to put in the effort to make it your own and adopt its practises.

H&S Check List - Your to-do list

1. Design salon with H&S in mind; consider fire escapes, ventilation, wires, lighting, cleaning etc. Consult with the H&S officer in your local council licensing department;
2. Create procedures for maintaining a hygienic and comfortable work environment
3. Do a complete substance inventory;
4. Identify those hazardous to health;
5. Perform risk assessments for all treatment processes, salon operations, equipment and substances (most of these will have safety data sheets);

 See chapter... ◎ Get it done 💡 Thinking time ■ Example ☺ You can do it!

6. Create procedures to mitigate the risks;
7. Make arrangements for first aid and accident recording;
8. Make arrangements for electrical checks;
9. Make arrangements for emergency evacuations, fire safety and the checking of fire safety equipment;
10. Train staff on these procedures.

Remember that even if you hire people with the correct qualifications; presumably professionals with experience and a good understanding of safe salon practises; every salon is different! You may be using a different brand of product to one they are use to; you may have a different set-up in terms of first aid and emergency evacuations. Go over all of your salon procedures with all your staff.

Licensing

Government business licensing is generally about setting minimum trading standards to ensure that the public are suitably protected against unsafe practises.

In some parts of the UK and for certain salon treatments a Special Treatments License is required. Find out if this is the case for your salon or chosen premises by calling the Health & Safety and Licensing departments of the local council or borough. It is crucial that you contact these authorities at the planning stages of your business and before you design your shop-fit as they may have special requirements to meet their criteria.

They will send you full details and information on what you must do or how to obtain the correct license for your business. This will probably include insurance, adequate H&S procedures, correct staff qualifications, etc.

Outside of the UK; ensure you find out what licensing is required in your area, especially in the US as this differs from state to state.

This is not optional!

Insurance

Insurance is about protecting yourself and your business from unforeseen incidences and is a must for any business; certainly for a salon. For this reason you want to make sure you get the right cover.

There are 2 types of insurance you should definitely get as an employer and a salon owner:-

- Employers Liability Compulsory Insurance; this one is for protection against claims from employees who may have suffered injuries or illness as a result of working for you.

- Public Liability Insurance; this one is for protection against claims from members of the public or customers who may have suffered injuries, illness or damage to their property caused by you or your business.

Other types of insurance cover you may need:-

- Buildings Insurance; the property your salon is in will need to be insured against damage. This is usually handled by the landlord of the property and you as the lease holder will have to pay towards it. You, of course, may be the landlord!

- Contents Insurance; this covers against damage or theft of stock, machinery, equipment and other content.

- Product Liability Insurance; if you sell or use products that have your business name on them you will need this insurance to cover you from any claims made as a result of injury or damage caused by your product.

- Property Owners' Liability Insurance; if you own the property, this insurance protects you against claims from members of the public who suffer injury as a result of an accident on your premises.

◎ Seek professional advice from an insurer or insurance broker about what cover is best for you and your business. You may not have to take out separate insurance policies for all the different types of insurance; usually all the cover you'll need is packaged into one policy.

Always check the details of your policy statements carefully and make sure you are properly covered!

Premiums & Excess

The premium is the cost of the insurance to you. This is usually paid per year, either in monthly instalments or as one lump sum.
The excess is an amount of money, paid by you, the policyholder, towards the claim. This is usually around the first £200 of a claim.

Keep your insurance premiums as low as possible by:-

- Having a good risk management policy; this means your H&S policies and procedures, good staff induction programmes and quality control measures, thereby minimising the risks of injury and damage.

- If you can afford it, pay your premium in one lump sum; most insurers offer discounts if you do this.

Finding An Insurer

Most big insurance companies offer a comprehensive range of business insurance options.

In beauty industry magazines, such as Scratch, Professional Beauty, Salon Business, Nail Pro, you will find companies offering insurance specifically designed for salons; whilst you should definitely get a quote from these companies I still recommend you seek out as many quotes from as many insurers as possible. Nevertheless, **the fact that they are offering salon specific packages means that they have an appetite for your particular business and are therefore likely to be the best priced options.**

 Always ensure that the broker or insurer you are dealing with is regulated by the Financial Services Authority. You can confirm this on their web site; www.fsa.gov.uk

More Information

Association of British Insurers Helpline
020 7600 3333

Association of Insurance and Risk Managers Enquiry Line
020 7480 7610

Business Link
www.businesslink.gov.uk

About.com

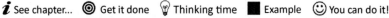

Chapter 16
PROFESSIONAL SERVICES
Accountants, Solicitors, Web designers & Shop-fitters

The professionals!

Why have I bothered to write a chapter on hiring professionals? You may be thinking – "Surely when I need an accountant, I can just use the Yellow Pages?" Yes, you can just use the yellow pages but having experienced the misfortune of not so professional professionals and/or not so transparent pricing policies, I believe this to be a very important money and time saving topic.

Beware...

As part of their marketing efforts, some professional service providers, such as accountancy firms, etc, will send recently registered companies, like yours, information on their services. This is above board as the address details of all registered companies are available to the public. However, you may be tempted to think that these businesses are somehow connected to Companies House and are therefore the best around and a good option for you. Please don't; they may be good, but there may be better out there... read on.

ACCOUNTANTS

What Do They Do And Why Do I Need One?

An accountant is a person formally trained to collect, record, analyse and communicate financial information. A professional accountant is one who has passed accountancy examinations and completed the required work experience.

As explained in *i* chapter 14 on Finance and Accounting, you will need an accountant to perform all or some of the following tasks:-

---

- Paying wages; generating payslips, P45's, P60's, PAYE
- Paying yourself; as above plus Self Assessment Returns
- PAYE calculations
- Self assessment tax returns
- Partnership tax returns
- VAT returns
- Bookkeeping
- End of year P&L accounts
- Corporation tax
- Balance sheet
- Paying dividends

Where Do I Find One?

You can find an accountant anywhere; online, in the phone book, etc; but I strongly advise using one that other business people have recommended to you. If you don't know anyone in business, pop into your local bakers, grocery store, printers, etc and ask them who they use! Get a handful of recommendations and meet them to have a chat.

Your tax and wages responsibilities as a business person are really important and you can not afford to have the wrong person in charge of your business accounts! There are a lot of dodgy, expensive, or just plain lazy and inefficient accountants out there, who instead of chasing you for your latest receipts and invoices, you're chasing them for payslips and tax returns!

As this is someone you will be in contact with quite regularly, ideally you want them to be local to your business. You don't want to have to travel too far or rely on the postal service to get your precious, priceless invoices and receipts to your accountant half way across town!

How Much Should They Cost?

An accountant in the UK, doing most of the services listed above for one salon and fewer than 6 employees should not cost you more than £900 per year. Try and stay away from accounting firms and find someone who works mostly on their own; they will be much more reasonably priced.

Personal experience...

Unfortunately the first accountants I used were introduced to me via the letterbox. They were local and respectable and as I didn't know any better, thought they must be a good option for my business. They were a firm of accountants with nice offices and great customer service. However, in the first year alone, when I had only 1 salon, their fees were £9,000 increasing to £11,000 in the second year!!! I had absolutely no idea that this could possibly be more than I needed to pay! They didn't say to me, "O, by-the-way Ego, your business may be too small for our type of firm, you may be better off using a smaller company." Nor did anyone else who looked at my business plan or advised me during those early years!

What a waste of money!

SOLICITORS / ATTORNEYS / LAWYERS

What Do They Do And Why Do I Need One?

A solicitor, attorney or lawyer (same thing) is a member of the legal profession qualified to advise clients on matters of the law.

The kinds of tasks you could need a solicitor for are:-

- Property matters; leases, purchases, etc
- Employment issues; staff contracts, disputes, tribunals, etc
- Company registration
- Partnership and shareholder agreements
- Drawing up of your will
- Any matters that may entail court hearings!

Where Do I Find One?

Again, like accountants, I advise going with a recommendation. The tasks of a solicitor are so varied, so for that reason choose one that has the specific experience that you need. For example, if it's the transference of a lease or a property purchase, get one that has done this before... well!

You can also find solicitors on the Law Society web site; visit www.lawsociety.org.uk

How Much Should They Cost?

Solicitors are not required on a regular basis and as such their fees vary depending on the job. On average, a solicitor's fees range from £100 – £250 per hour, so I suggest you get a quote for the whole job instead of paying an hourly rate. Be careful to ensure that the costs of any work done by a solicitor do not spiral out of control; keep your eye on them and their charging system! Don't be intimidated by lawyers, remember they are not necessarily smarter than you; they just have a different skill set!

Personal experience...

I once had a pair of solicitors quote me £2,000 for a job, clearly saying that in the worst case scenario their fees will not surpass £5,000.

This was already bad enough but the work needed to be done, so we went ahead. Unbelievably their final invoice came to £16,000!!! I was absolutely gob-smacked! When I asked for an understanding of how this could possibly be correct I was met with hostility and was told the hourly rate. I then demanded a breakdown of the hours, and again, unbelievably, was told that I would be charged extra for the time it will take for them to work-out the hours!! Absolutely outrageous!

Another waste of money!

GRAPHICS AND WEB DESIGNERS

What Do They Do And Why Do I Need One?

Graphics designers are the wonderfully creative people who design beautiful logos and create flawless looking artwork for leaflets, pricelists, adverts and other marketing material.

Professional and experienced graphics designers will use all the correct software applications, like Illustrator, Photoshop, InDesign, etc, to create unique marketing communications for your business.

Some businesses create their marketing material using Microsoft Word, PowerPoint or other inappropriate 'design' applications; whilst this might be a money saving option and possibly enough for certain things, most of the time the end result is obviously unprofessional. Refer to your marketing plan as to whether this is good enough for your business; otherwise, I strongly recommend that you have a professional create your business logo, pricelists, leaflets and web site.

You can and should find a graphics designer who is also a web designer. Granted there are some web jobs that require specialist technical people, but a good designer will know someone with the required skills and outsource those extra jobs on your behalf. Please don't have a visually second rate web site for your business; it just puts people off!

As mentioned in *i* chapter 13 on Marketing, it is very important to get the 'look and feel' of your business right!

Where Do I Find One?

One way of finding a good designer is by visiting the web sites that you really like; usually at the bottom of the pages there will be a link to the designer. Contact them and have a chat!

Another way is to advertise for one in local design colleges. They may not be that experienced but some of the students can be extremely talented individuals, eager to add work to their portfolios. This should be your most reasonably priced option.

Again, try and find an individual, not a company and make sure they show you what they have done in the past. Check that you both have the same taste/sorts of ideas; show them the kinds of logos, images and web sites you love and take it from there.

How Much Should They Cost?

This can vary greatly depending on who you get to do the work. Again I would stay away from the design companies, as they have higher overheads and therefore charge you more for their services.

The designers I know charge around £35 per hour. You may be able to get a better price than this, however sometimes it's just best to get them to quote for the whole job rather than charge you an hourly rate!

Logos usually cost around £200. Artwork for leaflets, pricelists, etc can cost from £60 upwards. Remember, printing costs are separate. Web sites cost anything from £400 depending on their complexity.

A good designer should design a few options for you to choose from and should be happy to make changes until you are satisfied. Make sure they provide your final logo as an eps file, which means it will not lose any of its sharpness no matter what size you print it. Also **make sure you have full ownership of your logo and any other products designed for you.**

SHOP-FITTERS, CONTRACTORS AND ARCHITECTS

What Do They Do And Why Do I Need One?

If you are going to have custom-built items made for your salon then you will probably need an architect and shop-fitter to design and make the items. Of course this is not necessary; if you don't have the budget for it then you can design and decorate your own salon yourself, as you would probably do for your own home. Who knows, you may be lucky to have a great eye for design and detail!

If you do have the budget for it, then using an Architect to design your shops layout is a great option. Like graphics designers they will create a complete look, using the whole salon space to full effect. You will have to give them a brief; providing them with the number of stations you require and all the correct dimensions for optimum workplace ergonomics (see *i* chapter 15, H&S), however they can also help you with this. Also, an experienced architect should already know and use a good contractor/builder/shop-fitter.

Some shop-fitters have in-house architects and shop designers. If they don't then you will need to know, pretty much to the last detail/dimension, how you want the shop finished.

Shop fitters that do offer interior design solutions as well as fit-out tend to be quite expensive but can be the perfect solution if you haven't got a clue where to start!

Personal experience...

Having owned 6 salons and needed to maintain a brand image throughout, I wanted to use people who could provide a consistent solution at a good price. My first couple of shops were created by a complete-solution shop fit company; they were the most expensive shops I had! Beautiful, but very costly! Finally I was introduced to a great architect who knew and had worked with a good contractor. I told him my budget and he designed and completed the next 4 shops within my budget! I paid a lot less for them and they were just as gorgeous!

Big lesson!

Where Do I Find One?

Online is probably the best resource but as with all jobs, get a few quotes and take it from there.

How Much Should They Cost?

That depends on your budget! Start all discussions at the lower end of your budget and see what you can get for your money.

Chapter 17
LAUNCH DAY!

Welcome one, welcome all!

It's Showtime!!

Well congratulations, by this stage you have no doubt been through the mill and the fun is only just about to begin! This is the day you have been working towards and probably secretly wish you could get a weeks sleep before you open! Well now it's **Showtime** and you have got to be at your very best...

PRE-LAUNCH

Firstly, in the build up to your salon opening make sure there is a sign telling people what's coming soon. When I say a sign, I don't mean a bit of A4 paper with tiny text, I mean have proper poster(s) printed with great bold text!

You could say things like "The best nail salon opening soon!" or "Top hair and beauty shop coming soon! It's just what you've been waiting for!"

Try to create some hype around the salon before it opens. See if you can get some local press write-ups about its launch. Whatever you have written or printed about you, blow-up and stick on your hoarding. This kind of thing can get local people talking and commenting about your business even before it starts! And then when it does open, they will just *have* to pay you a visit.

Other things to advertise before you open:-

- A short list of the most exciting treatments and services you will be offering.
- The opening date; announce it along with an opening day party or a 'meet and greet'!
- Your salon name; if the signage is ready, show it!
- Your salon web site; please only advertise this if it is actually ready for visits. Even if you haven't managed the full site, the

opening page should at least show a great logo, list of services, address, opening date, opening hours and a contact email.
- Opening hours.

Remember this is the beginning of your life in SALES! Display the type of information that is going to get your target market **excited**. Your marketing plan should steer you in the right direction.

Keep those who are interested in it, excited and eagerly awaiting the next bit of info!

PRE-LAUNCH PRESS DAY

It might be an idea to open the salon to the press and other VIPs first before opening to the public. This could be a Friday with a full launch planned for the Saturday. Send out invitations to every relevant editor, journalist and local celebrity you can find. Offer them the full list of treatments, especially the fast ones, along with drinks, canapés, lots of chat and a full press pack!

Obviously, the salon is in pristine condition; fully buffed and merchandised. Hire a professional photographer for the day to take photos of the salon, both empty and in full swing. Have your best sales people, even if they are your friends and family around; chatting and smiling with all the guests.

Make sure they get lots of information, have a great time and love the treatments.

Please bear in mind that it's not that easy to get press to come to events. You will have to be creative with your invitations, aim for the female journalists and follow-up invitations with phone calls. Refer to your marketing plan.

To ensure that you don't have an empty salon which can be

demoralising for you and the team; also invite local business people, the HR department of a local firm, owners of local complementary businesses, etc. to the party.

Make the most of this day as you don't know when you'll have this opportunity again once the salon opens!

OPEN FOR BUSINESS!

Here are some ideas for your launch:-

- Open on a Saturday

- If possible launch during the winter holiday season; this is party season and all beauty treatments are popular during party season!

- Don't launch in the summer; people are on holiday, out in the park or in their back gardens! If you must then it better be an express pedicure and waxing bar!

- Have an open day party; offer drinks, snacks and lots of chat, however make sure you are fully functional and able to take appointments.

- Use separate signage to invite people to browse the salon shop or just invite people in with some other enticing statements.

- Run a competition

Be creative!

And GOOD GOOD LUCK!!!!

Chapter 18
THE CHECK LIST
& NOTES

Is it all done?

Is it all done?

Use the check list below to help you keep track of where you are in
the process of Opening Your Own Salon!

Task	Thinking about it / Looking for it	Started it / Found it	½ way	Nearly!	Sorted!
Marketing plan					
Business plan					
Business bank account					
Premises (with sign!)					
Salon telephone lines					
Insurance					
License					
H&S Manual					
Business policies					
Interview process					
Staff starter pack; staff handbook and contracts					
Staff training program					
Staff!					
Salon operations sheets; rotas, paysheets, sales logs					
Accountant / Payroll					
Appointment system					
Comfortable and practical furniture					
Stock					
Equipment					
Pricelists					
Bins!					
3 months worth of promotions					

Your Paperwork At A Glance...

- Business Plan, including the financial forecasts
- Marketing Plan
- Staff Training Manual
- Staff Contract & Employment Manual or Handbook
- Salon Operations Manual
- Health & Safety Policy
- Health & Safety Procedures

NOTES...

NOTES...

NOTES...

NOTES...

Index

Index

Index

Index

Index

Index

Miss Salon™ Business Shop - www.misssalonbusiness.com

There are a number of salon-specific business tools available to purchase from Miss Salon™. See the list below and visit www.misssalon.com for more information.

A Completed Sample Business Plan £40.00* PDF
This is an actual business plan for a chain of nail bars that successfully raised £250k in loans and investment.

Sample Staff Handbook and Contract of Employment £9.99* PDF
Save yourself the time and effort of figuring out what to include and how to include it in your own staff handbook (employment manual); just tailor this sample to suit your salon!

Treatment and Product Pricing Calculator £24.99*
Microsoft Excel
This is an amazing Microsoft Excel spreadsheet; just input your salons direct and indirect costs and the calculator will work out what you need to charge for your services!

Profit & Loss Template £15.99* Microsoft Excel
Load your estimated or actual incomes and expenses into this template and it will create your P&L!

Cash Flow Template £15.99* Microsoft Excel
Just input what you spend, when you spend it and this dynamic template will keep you up-to-date on your cash situation. Also forecast your cash flow needs by including possible future spending.

Direct Costs Estimator Template £15.99* Microsoft Excel
Workout your businesses direct costs with this easy to use excel spreadsheet.

Health & Safety Policy Template £19.99* Microsoft Word
This is a H&S Policy used in a salon; just insert your business name

and details into this template. Every salon must have a H&S Policy.

Health & Safety Procedure Manual Template £24.99*
Microsoft Word
This H&S Procedure Manual, specifically designed for a salon, will save you the time and stress of producing your own from scratch. It contains all the required headings and sample content which you can easily replace with relevant statements about your salon.

Sample Health & Safety Induction £9.99* PDF
This Health & Safety Induction agenda is an excellent example of how a salons induction training session should be conducted.

Staff Performance Review Questionnaire £3.99* Microsoft Word
A complete performance review document created to assist you in conducting, the all important, formal staff assessments.

Sample Recruitment Interview Questions £3.99* Microsoft Word
A list of questions to definitely ask during an interview

Salon Inspection Sheet £3.99* Microsoft Word
A full salon inspection sheet with 10 questions that cover everything from appearance, to organisation, to staff participation

To purchase these products please visit www.misssalonbusiness.com or telephone our order and advice line on +44 (0)845 643 1619. They are available either on CD or via email.

*Prices may vary from those printed
All of the products are © Copyright 2008 Ego Iwegbu-Daley

Contact Ego Iwegbu-Daley

Write to me with your comments or questions...
misssalon@misssalon.com

Keep up to date with my blog...
www.misssalon.blogspot.com

View my latest videos...
www.youtube.com/misssalon

See my diary of events and join in on discussions...
Search for Miss Salon on facebook; www.facebook.com

If you have any problems with accessing these pages visit www.misssalon.com for easy links to all of our online information.

www.misssalon.com

Go confidently in the direction of your dreams!
Live the life you've imagined

- Thoreau

Lightning Source UK Ltd.
Milton Keynes UK
12 October 2010

161134UK00001B/94/P